# THE CAMBRIDGE BIBLE COMMENTARY
## NEW ENGLISH BIBLE

### GENERAL EDITORS
## P. R. ACKROYD, A. R. C. LEANEY, J. W. PACKER

# NEW TESTAMENT ILLUSTRATIONS

# NEW TESTAMENT ILLUSTRATIONS

Photographs, maps and diagrams
compiled and introduced by

## CLIFFORD M. JONES

*University of Leeds Institute of Education*

CAMBRIDGE
AT THE UNIVERSITY PRESS
1966

CAMBRIDGE UNIVERSITY PRESS
Cambridge, New York, Melbourne, Madrid, Cape Town, Singapore, São Paulo, Delhi

Cambridge University Press
The Edinburgh Building, Cambridge CB2 8RU, UK

Published in the United States of America by Cambridge University Press, New York

www.cambridge.org
Information on this title: www.cambridge.org/9780521054461

© Cambridge University Press 1966

First published 1966
Re-issued in this digitally printed version 2008

A catalogue record for this publication is available from the British Library

Library of Congress Catalogue Card Number: 66–10046

ISBN 978-0-521-05446-1 hardback
ISBN 978-0-521-09376-7 paperback

# GENERAL EDITORS' PREFACE

The aim of this series is to provide commentaries and other books about the Bible, based on the text of the New English Bible, and in these various volumes to make available to the general reader the results of modern scholarship. Teachers, and young people preparing for such examinations as the General Certificate of Education at Ordinary or Advanced Level in Britain and similar qualifications elsewhere, have been especially kept in mind. The commentators have been asked to assume no specialized theological knowledge, and no knowledge of Greek or Hebrew. Bare references to other literature and multiple references to other parts of the Bible have been avoided. Actual quotations have been given as often as possible.

This volume is designed to provide, in the form of maps, diagrams and photographs, information which will supplement the commentaries, giving in some detail, and in graphic form, material which can at best be briefly alluded to in that series. It is linked by its content with another volume—*Understanding the New Testament*—which outlines the larger historical background, says something about the growth and transmission of the text, and tries to answer the question 'Why should we study the New Testament?'. Both these volumes have been planned with the commentary series in mind, but are quite independent of it, and it is hoped that they will be useful to other readers as well.

P.R.A.

A.R.C.L.

J.W.P.

# AUTHOR'S NOTE

I am deeply grateful to the following for their assistance in the production of this book: the General Editors of *The Cambridge Bible Commentary* for their scrupulous criticism of the manuscript and their many suggestions for its improvement; the editorial staff of the Cambridge University Press, for advice on artistic matters and help with the details of production; the Reverend H. St J. Hart, Queens' College, Cambridge, for his skilful photography of the coins (**95** to **107**) and for much useful information about them; Dr Kathleen Kenyon, St Hugh's College, Oxford, for a photograph of Jericho (**44**) and her comments on it; Mr D. R. Ap-Thomas, University College of North Wales, Bangor, for advice on the topography of Jerusalem (**191**).

Old Testament quotations are from the Revised Version, and New Testament quotations are from the New English Bible.

Map references to places will be found in the Index of Subjects.

C.M.J.

# CONTENTS

# ACKNOWLEDGEMENTS

The author and publishers are grateful to the following for permission to reproduce photographs. Photographs acknowledged to Alinari, Anderson and Brogi have been supplied by the Mansell Collection, London. The assistance of Illustrations Research Service, London, is also gratefully acknowledged.

1. B.B.C. Publications, London; 2. Fr. Luc Grollenberg O.P.; 3. Nuellens, Aachen; 4, 5. Anderson; 6. Brogi; 7. British Museum; 8, 9. Alinari; 10. Middle East Archives; 11. Hebrew University of Jerusalem; 12. Turkish Embassy, 43 Belgrave Square, S.W.1; 13. Willem van de Poll; 14. Paul Popper; 15. J. Allan Cash; 16. Lala Aufsberg, Sonthofen im Allgäu; 17. American School of Classical Studies, Athens; 18. Anderson; 19. Lala Aufsberg; 20. J. Allan Cash; 21. Royal Institute of British Architects: Sir Banister Fletcher Library (after Dinsmoor); 22. British Museum; 23, 24. J. Allan Cash; 25. Alinari; 26. Anderson; 27. A. F. Kersting; 28. Matson Photo Service, Los Angeles; 29. Willem van de Poll; 30. Agence Rapho, Paris; 31. Willem van de Poll; 32. Radio Times Hulton Picture Library; 33. Paul Popper; 34. Camera Press, London; 35. Willem van de Poll; 36. Paul Popper; 37, 38. Willem van de Poll; 39. Palestine Exploration Fund; 40, 41, 42. Willem van de Poll; 43. Radio Times Hulton Picture Library; 44. Dr Kathleen Kenyon; 45, 46. Willem van de Poll; 47. Matson Photo Service; 48. Camera Press, London; 49. Willem van de Poll; 50. Willem van de Poll; 52. Matson Photo Service; 53. J. Allan Cash; 54, 55, 56. Willem van de Poll; 57. Paul Popper; 58. J. Allan Cash; 59. Paul Popper; 60, 61, 62. Willem van de Poll; 63. Ashmolean Museum; 64, 65. Willem van de Poll; 66. Matson Photo Service; 67. Radio Times Hulton Picture Library; 68. Willem van de Poll; 69. Radio Times Hulton Picture Library; 70, 71. Matson Photo Service; 72, 73. Camera Press, London; 74. Willem van de Poll; 75. Matson Photo Service; 76. Middle East Archives; 77. Willem van de Poll; 78. *Jewish Chronicle*; 79. Paul Popper; 80. Willem van de Poll; 81. Willem van de Poll; 82. John R. Freeman & Co.; 83. *Jewish Chronicle*; 84, 85. Willem van de Poll; 86. American School of Oriental Research and John R. Freeman & Co.; 87. Radio Times Hulton Picture Library; 89. Hebrew University of Jerusalem (after Sukenik); 90. Willem van de Poll; 91. Paul Popper; 92. Copyright: Ecole Biblique et Archéologique Française de Jérusalem; 93. Youth Aliyah Organization; 94. *Jewish Chronicle*; 95–107. The Rev. H. St J. Hart; 108. *The Times*, London; 109. J. Allan Cash; 110, 111. John Rylands Library, Manchester; 112. Staatliche Museen zu Berlin; 113–117. British Museum; 118. Vatican Library; 119. Chester Beatty Library; 120–124. British Museum; 125. Radio Times Hulton Picture Library; 126. British Museum; 127. Radio Times Hulton Picture Library; 128. British and Foreign Bible Society; 129. Radio Times Hulton Picture Library; 130. British and Foreign Bible Society; 132. British Museum; 133. Anderson; 134. Victoria and Albert Museum; 135. St Matthew's Church, Northampton; 136. Museum of Medieval Austrian Art, Vienna; 137. Edita S. A., Lausanne; 138. City of Birmingham; 139. National Gallery, London; 140. Edita S. A., Lausanne; 141. British Museum; 142. Cleveland Museum of Art, Ohio (gift of the Hanna Fund); 143. Willem van de Poll; 144. Mansell Collection; 145. D. W. Tooth, 31 Bruton Street, W.1; 146. Tate Gallery, London; 147. Thompson, Coventry; 148. British Museum; 149. Edita S. A., Lausanne; 150. Giraudon; 151. Felix H. Man, London; 152. Alinari; 153. Mansell Collection; 154. Stanley Travers, Cardiff; 155, 156. A.C.L., Brussels; 157, 158. Thompson, Coventry; 159. Bavarian State Art Collection, Munich; 160. Anderson; 161. Alinari; 162. National Gallery, London; 163. British Museum; 164. Thompson, Coventry; 165. Pontifical Commission for Sacred Art, Rome; 167, 168. Anderson; 172. Alinari; 173–6. University Library, Cambridge; 178. Pontifical Commission for Sacred Art; 179. John R. Freeman & Co.; 180. National Buildings Record; 182. Museum, Cirencester.

The main reason for reading the New Testament is to discover what Christianity is about, but many people never make the discovery because they do not understand the New Testament when they read it. For them, reading the New Testament is like going to the theatre to see a play and then finding that the scenery, the dress, the speech and the behaviour of the actors are all completely strange and unfamiliar. To appreciate the play it is necessary to understand its setting and to know something about the background of the plot. Similarly, those who wish to understand the New Testament must be familiar with the historical, geographical, social and religious situation that existed in the Mediterranean world in the New Testament period.

This book is intended to accompany and to supplement the volumes of the *Cambridge Bible Commentary*. It contains material to illustrate the background of the New Testament, and this material is mainly pictorial because we take more notice of pictures, learn more from them, and remember them better than either the written or the spoken word. The material is of three kinds: (1) photographs, (2) maps and plans, (3) charts and diagrams.

The photographs are in two groups. The first group contains pictures of places or objects associated with the New Testament. The camera was not invented until the early years of the nineteenth century, so that photography of New Testament subjects is necessarily restricted to those objects that have been preserved from ancient times and those places still in existence that are mentioned in the New Testament. In both cases we are extremely fortunate. The hot dry conditions of much of the Near East have remarkably preserved the documents, the household and religious articles of everyday life, and the buildings of New Testament times; and archaeologists have been able to recover many of these for us in recent years. Equally fortunate from our point of view is the fact that life in the Near East has remained almost unchanged until very recently. The photographs reproduced in this book therefore give some idea of the appearance in the first century of the places they depict. By studying the illustrations it ought to be possible to visualize the world in which Jesus and his followers lived, the everyday scenes with which they were familiar, and the objects they used in their daily work and worship, and so to get a better understanding of the background against which the New Testament was written.

The second group of photographs contains reproductions of works of art. There are in the world many thousands of pictures devoted to Christian subjects, but there is room in a small book like this for photographs of only a few of them. This is not, in any case, a book on great art or a collection of the world's most famous pictures, but a pictorial commentary on the New Testament. It ought therefore to reflect the religious spirit of the New Testament, and by no means all great works of art do that, even though they depict Christian subjects. A picture may be artistically magnificent but religiously almost worthless; but some artists have managed to make Christian truth shine through their work and to make it shine so clearly that all may recognize it. If an artist has been able to do this, his picture is suitable for inclusion in this book. The decision to include some works of art and to exclude others must of course be to some extent a personal matter, and it is likely that there will be disagreement about some of the decisions made. In matters of art and religious insight this is inevitable.

There is one exception to all this. Occasionally a picture has been included not because it is great art and not because it shows deep spiritual insight, but because the artist has been at pains to make the details of his picture as authentic as possible. Nevertheless, authentic detail of this kind need not always be looked for in Christian art. A picture is not to be despised because the artist uses his own background for the scenes of New Testament incidents: a Dutch stable for the Nativity, an Italian dining-room for the Last Supper, a Spanish hillside for the Crucifixion, or a Thames-side churchyard for the Resurrection. Nor need a picture fail to display Christian truth because a Chinese artist chooses to show Jesus with a pigtail, or an African artist to show him with a black face. These are minor matters compared with the artist's ability to communicate religious truth to those who look at his pictures.

A few signs and symbols are illustrated. Christian symbolism has its source in the New Testament, and the symbols themselves are frequently seen in churches today, but for many people they have little or no meaning. The sign of the hammer and sickle speaks more clearly to most people in the modern world than does the sign of the fish or even the sign of the cross. Nevertheless, for a true understanding of the Christian faith an insight into the meaning of Christian signs and symbols is essential.

The charts and diagrams reproduced here are intended to summarize information in a graphic way and to show at a glance something that would take a long time to read if it were described in words. While it is true that the broad meaning of a diagram can usually be seen at once, closer study will often show it to contain more information than was obvious at first.

Although this collection of illustrations has been compiled with the *Cambridge Bible Commentary* in mind, it can equally well be used with any other standard commentary, or indeed by those who prefer to study the New Testament without reference to a commentary. It has two indexes: an index of subjects and an index of texts. If one or other of these indexes is consulted the reader will often be helped to understand a difficult passage or enabled to visualize an incident, a place or an object, and so to get a better grasp of the subject being studied.

# The Background of the
# New Testament

1 *Roman standard*

# 1 HISTORICAL:
# THE GRECO-ROMAN WORLD

## THE ROMAN EMPIRE

The conquests of Alexander the Great in the fourth century B.C. brought about the decline and the eventual fall of the Persian Empire, and Greek rule was established from the Sahara Desert to the Indian Ocean. Greek became the common language of the civilized world and Greek culture made its influence felt everywhere. In its turn, Greek power waned and was succeeded by Roman rule. In 63 B.C. Jerusalem was captured by Pompey, a Roman general, and Judaea became part of the Roman province of Syria. A map showing the extent of the Roman Empire will be found numbered **184** (p. 158).

From this time and until long after the New Testament period, Palestine was an enemy-occupied country, and as a sign of Roman occupation a standard like this (**1**) was set up in public buildings and in the streets of the towns and villages of Judaea. The Romans usually respected the religious scruples of the Jews and did not take the standard into sacred places. The laurel wreath stands for victory, the eagle for power, and the letters SPQR for *Senatus Populusque Romanus* (The Roman Senate and People).

## ROMAN MILESTONE

A Roman mile was 4860 English feet, or about 12/13ths of an English mile. Milestones (**2**) were set up on the main roads and distances were measured from the large towns. It was rare for the milestones to have mileage figures marked on them.

A 'man in authority' (Matt. 5 : 41), i.e. a Roman government official or a Roman

**2** *Roman milestone: Transjordan*

soldier, could compel a non-Roman subject to carry his baggage or equipment for 1 mile along the road. Jesus's recommendation to his followers to offer the Romans twice as much service as was legally necessary would not please the anti-Roman zealots; but 'going the second mile', understood metaphorically, is the essence of Christian action.

### ROMAN EMPERORS

At first Rome was ruled by a king, but when Rome became a republic, authority passed into the hands of a few aristocratic families. Julius Caesar seized power during the century before the New Testament period, but he was murdered by his enemies in 44 B.C. and civil war broke out. Eventually Octavian had himself proclaimed emperor and the Roman Empire came into being. The emperors who held office during the New Testament period are listed in the time-chart (**194**). Coins bearing impressions of the emperors are described and illustrated on p. 91.

*Augustus* (**3**) was the title given to Octavian (the Latin word *augustus* means majestic, dignified), and it was during his reign that, according to Luke, there was 'a general registration throughout the Roman world' in which 'everyone made his way to his own town'. Mary and Joseph went to Bethlehem 'to be registered', and it was while they were there that Mary 'gave birth to a son, her first-born' (Luke 2:1–7).

3 *Augustus* (27 B.C.–A.D. 14): *cameo set in a cross in the Treasury of Aachen Cathedral, Germany*

*Tiberius* (**4**) was the second Roman emperor, and it was in 'the fifteenth year' of his reign (i.e. A.D. 28), 'when Pontius Pilate was governor of Judaea', that John 'announced the good news' of the coming of the Messiah (Luke 3 : 1–18). Tiberius was the Roman emperor during the ministry of Jesus. Tiberias (**34**), a town on the shores of the Sea of Galilee, was built in his honour and named after him by Herod Antipas.

**5** (*Above*) *Claudius* (41–54): *Vatican, Rome*

**4** (*Left*) *Tiberius* (14–37): *Vatican, Rome*

*Claudius* (**5**) was a nephew of Tiberius and the fourth Roman emperor. At first he was friendly to the Jews, but later he 'issued an edict that all Jews should leave Rome' (Acts 18 : 2). 'A severe and world-wide famine' occurred during his reign. It brought much suffering to the Christians in Judaea, and the record of it includes an account of one of the earliest examples of famine relief (Acts 11 : 27–30).

*Nero* (**6**) was the adopted son of Claudius and the fifth Roman emperor. He is not mentioned by name in the New Testament, but he is the one described as 'Emperor' (Acts 25: 8), 'Caesar' (Acts 25: 12), or 'His Imperial Majesty' (Acts 25: 21) in the account of Paul's appeal for a fair trial. Nero was the first great persecutor of the Church and if his portraits truly represent him, his appearance is an indication of his cruel nature. He is probably the emperor referred to as 'the beast' whose name has 'the numerical value . . . six hundred and sixty-six' (Rev. 13: 18). 'Numerical value' in this quotation means the total reached by adding together the numbers corresponding to the letters in the words Nero Caesar written in Hebrew.

6 *Nero (54–68): Uffizi, Florence*    7 *Titus (79–81): British Museum, London*

Nero authorized *Vespasian*, afterwards emperor, to put down a Jewish rebellion in Judaea, and terrible slaughter took place in Galilee. Jerusalem was not captured until A.D. 70, and it was *Titus* (**7**), Vespasian's son and eventually emperor, who conducted the campaign. A triumphal arch was built in the Forum at Rome (it is still to be seen) to commemorate the victory. This detail (**8**) from the arch of Titus shows loot from Herod's temple being carried in procession. Notice the laurel wreaths worn by the victors, the seven-branched candlestick which stood in the holy of holies in the temple according to Exod. 25: 31–9, and the trumpets.

Domitian (**9**) was the second great persecutor of the Church ('a second Nero'), and according to the historian Eusebius it was during his reign that John, the author of the Revelation, was banished to 'the island called Patmos' (Rev. 1 : 9).

**9** *Domitian* (81–96): *Museo Capitolino, Rome*

GOVERNORS OF JUDAEA

Archelaus, the most hated of Herod's sons (p. 169), was banished from the throne following complaints about his misrule and Judaea came under the authority of governors appointed by Rome. These officials lived at Caesarea on the Mediterranean coast and visited Jerusalem only when their presence was necessary. The governors who ruled in Judaea during the New Testament period are listed in the time-chart (**194**).

The first governor took office in A.D. 6, but it is the fifth governor of Judaea, Pontius Pilate, who ruled from A.D. 26 to 36, whose name is most familiar. He was a ruthless official who played a miserable part in the trial of Jesus. He was removed from office for the inefficiency of his rule, and tradition says that he ended his life by suicide.

During excavations by some Italian archaeologists in June 1961 in the Roman theatre at Caesarea (**59**) a stone slab was unearthed (**10**). A Latin inscription on the stone records the dedication of a building in honour of the emperor Tiberius (**4**), and mentions by name the governor of Judaea, Pontius Pilate. The word *Pilatus* and part of the word *Pontius* can be distinguished on the second line of the inscription. This is an important find, for it is the first known occurrence of the name of Pilate in an ancient inscription.

**10** *Inscription found in the Roman theatre, Caesarea*

**11** *Inscription found in the Ophel Synagogue, Jerusalem*

## HELLENISTS

Many of the Jews who left Palestine to live in other parts of the world eventually forgot their native language and learned to speak Greek instead. They were called Hellenists, 'Greek-speaking Jews' (Acts 9: 29) or 'those . . . who spoke Greek' (Acts 6: 1). Stephen, one of the 'seven men of good reputation' chosen to supervise the daily distribution of bread to the widows of Hellenists in Jerusalem, was probably a Hellenist himself who had come from abroad to live in Jerusalem (Acts 6: 1–6).

This Greek inscription (**11**) was once in a Hellenist synagogue in Jerusalem. It tells how a priest called Theodotus built a synagogue and a hostel for foreigners in the city.

## TARSUS

Tarsus was the chief city of the Roman province of Cilicia and the residence of the governor. It was 12 miles from the sea on the banks of the river Cydnus, and was noted for its fine schools. This photograph of the modern city (**12**) shows the Taurus Mountains in the far distance and a school in the foreground.

Paul was born at Tarsus and he was proud to call himself 'a Tarsian from Cilicia, a citizen of no mean city' (Acts 21 : 39). He says he was 'brought up in this city', but 'this' probably refers to the city of Jerusalem and not Tarsus. He was 'a pupil of Gamaliel' (Acts 22 : 3), whom Luke describes as 'a member of the Council . . . a Pharisee . . . a teacher of the law held in high regard by all the people' (Acts 5 : 34).

**12** *Tarsus*

**13** *Damascus: Straight Street*

## DAMASCUS

Damascus was the ancient capital of Syria, the kingdom to the north of Palestine. The city was reconstructed in the Greek period by Hippodamus, a famous town-planner. He gave it a rectangular boundary and made its streets straight and at right angles to one another. The longest of these streets, running east–west through the city, was called Straight Street. It is more than a mile long and it is still the main street in the old part of Damascus (**13**). In Paul's day it was a magnificent avenue with noble pillars and fine archways. The house of Judas where Paul stayed following his experience 'on the road and nearing Damascus' was in Straight Street (Acts 9: 1-19).

ANTIOCH

Antioch (**14**) was the capital of the Roman province of Syria. It lies at the foot of Mount Silpius, from the summit of which this photograph is taken and on which the citadel once stood. The river Orontes can be seen across the middle of the picture. In the period of Acts, Antioch was the third largest city in the Roman Empire, only Rome and Alexandria being larger. It is 15 miles inland from the coast and Seleucia is its port. Paul and Barnabas 'sent out on their mission by the Holy Spirit, came down to Seleucia' (Acts 13 : 4). It was at Antioch that the mission to the Gentiles began, for here the followers of Jesus 'began to speak to pagans as well, telling them the good news of the Lord Jesus' (Acts 11 : 20). It was here also that 'the disciples first got the name of Christians' (Acts 11 : 26).

There was another town called Antioch, in the Roman province of Galatia. It is called 'Pisidian Antioch' in Acts 13 : 14, but 'Antioch' in Acts 14 : 19–21 and 2 Tim. 3 : 11.

**14** *Antioch*

**15** *Athens: the Acropolis*

## ATHENS

The ancient city of Athens grew round the hill called Acropolis (i.e. the highest point of the city). This rocky crag rising 300 feet above its surroundings is seen in the middle of the picture (**15**). Several temples were built on its summit in the days when Greece was at the zenith of her fame, chief among them the Parthenon, the temple of Athena, a magnificent structure of splendid proportions and great beauty. Its ruins can be seen in the picture, crowning the Acropolis. Some of its sculptured friezes are now in the British Museum and are known as the Elgin Marbles, named after the Earl of Elgin who brought them to England in 1812.

Paul visited Athens during the course of his second missionary journey. He was no doubt impressed by its great beauty, but he was also 'exasperated to see how the city was full of idols' (Acts 17: 16).

**16** *Athens: the Areopagus*

The Areopagus is a huge lump of white limestone which stands as a landmark a short distance north-west of the Acropolis in Athens (**16**). The Greek word Areopagus means 'the hill of Ares', and Ares is the Greek name for Mars, the god of war. The hill is therefore sometimes called Mars' Hill. An impression of its size is gained by comparing it with the people climbing on it and the coaches parked at the foot of it in the picture.

Mars' Hill served in ancient Athens as an open-air court, and some of the 'philosophers' of Athens brought Paul before 'the Court of Areopagus' and questioned him about the 'new doctrine' he was proclaiming (Acts 17: 18–21). 'Some scoffed' at his teaching, but others 'joined him and became believers' (Acts 17: 32–4). Paul also discussed religious questions in the local synagogue and 'in the city square every day with casual passers-by' (Acts 17: 17). This 'city square' was the Agora, which is situated a short distance north-west of the Areopagus. It has been excavated by American archaeologists and one side of it, the Stoa of Attalos, has been restored to its original appearance (**17**). Parts of some of the original pillars can be seen in front of the restored colonnade, and the towering height of the Acropolis is in the background. The Stoa was a covered walk used as a promenade or meeting place, and it was famous because Zeno taught there in the third century B.C. A fine museum of objects excavated in the locality is housed in the Stoa today.

**17** *Athens: the Agora*

During his visit to Athens Paul made a tour of the city and he says he 'noticed among other things an altar bearing the inscription "To an Unknown God"' (Acts 17: 23). No altar bearing this inscription has ever been found in Athens, but altars bearing a similar inscription have been found elsewhere. The altar illustrated here (**18**) is thought to date from about 100 B.C. The inscription says the altar is 'sacred to a god' and that it was restored by Sextius and Calvinus.

**18** *Altar to an unknown god: Palatine Hill, Rome*

**19** *Corinth: Acro-Corinthus and Temple of Apollo*

## CORINTH

Paul called at Corinth on his second missionary journey. It was originally a Greek city built on an isthmus at the foot of Acro-Corinthus, a mountain which had a temple at its summit. Following a disastrous fire, the city was rebuilt by Julius Caesar in 46 B.C. and it became the capital of the Roman province of Achaia. One photograph (**19**) shows the ruins of the Temple of Apollo, with the Acro-Corinthus in the background, and another (**20**) shows the view overlooking the Gulf of Corinth from the summit of the Acro-Corinthus.

During his stay in the city Paul met a Jew called Aquila and his wife, Priscilla, tent-makers like himself, and 'he made his home with them, and they carried on business together' (Acts 18: 1–4). He preached first in the synagogue, then in 'the house of a worshipper of God named Titius Justus, who lived next door to the synagogue' (Acts 18: 5–7).

**20** *Corinth: Gulf of Corinth from Acro-Corinthus*

**21** *Ephesus: a reconstruction of the Temple of Diana*

EPHESUS

Ephesus was an important seaport on the west coast of Asia Minor, and its Temple of Diana was one of the seven wonders of the ancient world. The magnificence of the temple may be judged from this reconstruction of its probable appearance in the fourth century B.C. (**21**) and from the richly sculptured base of one of its pillars now in the British Museum (**22**). The remains of a marble-paved street and the porch of the Temple of Hadrian (**23**) show how fine a city Ephesus was in Paul's day.

**22** *Ephesus: base of a pillar from the Temple of Diana: British Museum, London*

**23** *Ephesus: marble street and ruins of the Temple of Hadrian*

When Paul visited Ephesus 'the Christian movement gave rise to a serious disturbance' which centred round 'the sanctuary of the great goddess Diana' (Acts 19: 23–41). The scene of this uproar was 'the theatre' (Acts 19: 29), the ruins of which are seen in this picture (**24**). The semi-circular area was the stage and the photograph is taken from the rising ground on which the audience sat.

Diana, whose Greek name was Artemis, was the mother-goddess of Asia Minor, and the falling to earth of a meteorite roughly in the shape of a woman with outstretched arms and many breasts may have given rise to the commonly held belief ('all the world knows') that it was a 'symbol' of Diana that had fallen from heaven (Acts 19: 35). 'Silver shrines of Diana' were manufactured by the local craftsmen for the pilgrims who flocked to worship her in the temple at Ephesus (Acts 19: 24), and images of the goddess continued to be made long after the time of Paul. Representations of many other gods can be seen in relief on this statuette of Diana (**25**).

**25** *Diana: marble statue of the goddess: Museo Conservatori, Rome*

**24** *Ephesus: the theatre*

**26** *Appian Way*

## THE APPIAN WAY

The Appian Way (**26**) was a famous and much-travelled road running south-east from Rome to Capua. It was named after its builder in the fourth century B.C., Appius Claudius Caecus (i.e. Blind Appius Claudius). The Christians of Rome came out along the Appian Way to greet Paul as he neared the end of his journey, meeting him at Appii Forum (i.e. the market-place of Appius), an ancient town about 40 miles from Rome (Acts 28 : 15).

**27** *Patmos: view from the hill near the Monastery of St John*

PATMOS

Patmos is a rocky island, about 10 miles long by 6 miles wide, off the west coast of Asia Minor. The Romans used this barren rock as a penal settlement to which they sent political agitators and any who threatened the peace of the empire. By order of the emperor, John, the author of the Revelation (**162**), was banished to 'the island called Patmos' (Rev. 1 : 9).

The monastery of St John stands on a hill on the island. It was built in the eleventh century and it houses a rich collection of religious objects and many valuable manuscripts, including 33 pages of the Red Codex, so called because it is written in letters of gold and silver on red parchment. The illustration (**27**) shows the view from a point near the monastery.

## 2 GEOGRAPHICAL:
## PLACES IN THE HOLY LAND

### BETHLEHEM

Although it was not much more than a village in size, Bethlehem was regarded by one of the prophets (Mic. 5: 2) as 'far from least in the eyes of the rulers of Judah', because it was the place where 'a leader to be the shepherd of . . . Israel' would be born (Matt. 2: 4–6). Both Matthew and Luke name Bethlehem as the birthplace of Jesus (Matt. 2: 1; Luke 2: 4–7). Matthew also records Herod's horrible crime, 'the massacre of all children in Bethlehem and its neighbourhood, of the age of two years or less' (Matt. 2: 16).

Modern Bethlehem is about five miles south of Jerusalem, and this photograph (**28**) shows a view of the city from the south-west. Notice the profusion of spring flowers in the foreground ('even Solomon in all his splendour was not attired like one of these'; Matt. 6: 29), and the tall church tower on the skyline which stands near the traditional place of Jesus's birth.

**28** *Bethlehem: view from the south*

**29** *Nazareth*

NAZARETH

Nazareth (**29**) lies in an elevated saucer from the rim of which there is a fascinating view in every direction (see also **61**). Jesus lived in Nazareth as a boy and it was here that he 'grew big and strong and full of wisdom' (Luke 2 : 40). When he was older he returned to Nazareth one week-end and preached in the synagogue there. His sermon was such that 'the whole congregation were infuriated' by it, and they tried to throw him over the 'brow of the hill' on which Nazareth was built (Luke 4 : 16–30).

QUMRAN

Qumran is a short distance from the north-western shore of the Dead Sea, and this illustration (**30**) shows the ruins of a settlement that was there in the time of Christ. The occupants of the settlement at that time are thought to have been a pious group called the Essenes, who were specially interested in ceremonial washings and whose library, which contained the Qumran scrolls, often called the Dead Sea scrolls (**86**), has been discovered in recent years hidden in caves in the near-by cliffs. Some scholars believe that the teaching of John the Baptist originated at Qumran, and some even suggest that John may have been a member of the community there.

**30** *Qumran: ruins of the settlement*

THE WILDERNESS

The 'wilderness' mentioned in the gospels (it is also called 'the Judaean wilderness': Matt. 3: 1; and 'the open pasture': Luke 15: 4) is not the desert in the extreme south and east of Palestine, but the mountainous area west of the Jordan valley (**33**). It was in this barren, inhospitable region that Jesus 'for forty days was led by the Spirit up and down . . . and tempted by the devil' (Luke 4: 1–13).

This type of country can be seen in the photograph (**31**) taken from the mound (in the foreground) which marks the site of the ancient city of Jericho. The flat-topped height near the middle of the picture is known as the Mount of Temptation (**76**). The monastery half-way up was built to commemorate Christ's forty days of temptation in this dreary wilderness.

**31** *The wilderness: Mount of Temptation in the distance*

**32** *River Jordan: one of its sources near Caesarea Philippi*

### THE RIVER JORDAN

A number of small streams unite to form the source of the river Jordan, one of them an underground stream which comes out of a hole in the cliff face near Caesarea Philippi (**32**). Lake Huleh, shown on some old maps, has now been drained and the river follows a winding course for 12½ miles from its source to the Sea of Galilee, falling on the way from about 1000 feet above sea-level at Caesarea Philippi to 682 feet below sea-level at the Sea of Galilee. From the southern end of the Sea of Galilee to the Dead Sea, which is 1292 feet below sea-level, the river flows through a narrow valley some 65 miles long, twisting and turning in a jungle of trees, bushes and tangled undergrowth (**33**). At one of the more placid stretches of the river crowds flocked to be baptized by John, 'confessing their sins' (Matt. 3 : 5–6). Jesus also was baptized, 'the Spirit of God descending like a dove to alight upon him' (Matt. 3 : 13–17). Artists have often tried to portray this incident (e.g. **139** and **140**).

**33** *River Jordan: view from the air*

**34** *Sea of Galilee: view from the hill above Tiberias*

### THE SEA OF GALILEE

The Sea of Galilee is a beautiful inland lake, 12 miles long and 8 miles wide at its widest part, surrounded on all sides by low hills which are pierced by narrow gorges here and there. It is sometimes called the Sea of Tiberias (John 6: 1; 21: 1) from the name of a town on its west shore; or the Lake of Gennesaret (Luke 5: 1), perhaps from the Hebrew word for a harp (*chinnor:* 'the sea of Chinneroth'; Josh. 12: 3), the lake being roughly harp-shaped. Tiberias, the only town on the shores of the lake today, is the cluster of houses seen at the foot of the hill from which this photograph (**34**) is taken. There is no record in the gospels that Jesus ever visited it. In New Testament times there was a girdle of towns round the lake. Capernaum was near the northern end of the lake, and its site is on the extreme left of the picture. These towns were the centres of a considerable fishing, boat-building and fish-curing industry, and there was a great deal of agricultural activity where the trees had been cleared from the land near the shore. Tradition says that Jesus spoke the Beatitudes on the slopes of the hill at the northern end of the Sea of Galilee, and it was from the region round the lake that he chose some of his disciples. Four of them who were fishermen were called by Jesus as he was 'walking by the Sea of Galilee' (Matt. 4: 18–22), and it was in this area that 'great crowds gathered to hear him and to be cured of their ailments' (Luke 5: 15). Sometimes a storm arises unexpectedly on the Sea of Galilee (**35**), and small boats are in danger of being swamped. A well-known incident recorded in the gospels says that 'all at once a great storm arose on the lake, till the waves were breaking right over the boat' (Matt. 8: 23–7).

**35** *Sea of Galilee: a storm*

CAPERNAUM

The magnificent ruins, seen from the air (**36**) and at close quarters (**37**), are those of a synagogue standing on the north-west shore of the Sea of Galilee on a site probably occupied by Capernaum in Christ's time. The synagogue is of the period near the end of the second or the beginning of the third century, but it probably stands on the same ground as the synagogue which was the gift of the centurion in command of the local

**36** *Capernaum: ruins of the synagogue from the air*

garrison, of whom the Jewish elders said to Jesus: 'He is a friend of our nation and it is he who built us our synagogue' (Luke 7: 5). It may be that Jesus preached in the earlier synagogue on this site. The richness of the carving on the stones in the illustration (**37**) gives some idea of the splendour of the synagogue at Capernaum in its heyday.

**37** *Capernaum: ruins of the synagogue*

**38** *Chorazin: ruins of the synagogue*

## CHORAZIN

Matthew lists three towns visited by Jesus 'in which most of his miracles had been performed'. They are Bethsaida, Chorazin and Capernaum. In spite of the signs they had been privileged to see, the inhabitants of these places remained unmoved, and Jesus 'denounced them for their impenitence' (Matt. 11 : 20–4).

Chorazin was near the shore of the Sea of Galilee, a short distance from Capernaum. Its synagogue, of the third or fourth century, was built of black basalt and almost certainly stood on the site of the synagogue in which Jesus may have preached. It has recently been excavated (**38**).

**39** *Bethany*

BETHANY

Bethany (**39**) is a small town 'just under two miles from Jerusalem' (John 11 : 18) on the eastern slope of the Mount of Olives (**48**) on the road to Jericho. The illustration shows a typical Palestinian scene, and the flat-roofed houses are very much as they must have been in Jesus's time. Bethany was the home town of Mary, Martha and Lazarus, and of 'Simon the leper' (Mark 14 : 3). Perhaps because he was friendly with Mary and Martha and Lazarus, Jesus often went to Bethany, and it was to Bethany that he took his disciples for the last act of his ministry and then 'parted from them' (Luke 24 : 50–1).

SAMARIA

Samaria occupies a fine site at the top of a hill. It was built by Omri (1 Kings 16 : 24) and became the capital of the northern kingdom of Israel. It was rebuilt by Herod the Great and renamed Sebaste in honour of the first Roman emperor, Augustus (*Sebastos* in Greek). Herod adorned it with a magnificent temple, a fine stadium where games were held every five years, and a number of other buildings of great splendour. An example of Herod's work excavated at Samaria is seen in this picture (**40**).

The name Samaria is also given to the territory sandwiched between Galilee in the north and Judaea in the south (John 4 : 3–4). The positions of the city and the territory can be seen on the map (**186**).

**40** *Samaria: ruins of Herod's city*

**41** *Mount Gerizim*

## MOUNT GERIZIM

Gerizim is not mentioned by name in the New Testament, but it is almost certainly the hill referred to by the Samaritan woman when she said to Jesus: 'Our fathers worshipped on this mountain, but you Jews say that the temple where God should be worshipped is in Jerusalem' (John 4: 20). A Samaritan temple had been built on the summit of Gerizim in the fourth century B.C., and although it was destroyed by John Hyrcanus, a nephew of Judas Maccabaeus, in 128 B.C., this did not prevent the Samaritans in Christ's time, any more than it prevents Samaritans today, from continuing to worship on the same hilltop. This photograph (**41**) shows the hill rising 700 feet above Nablus (ancient Shechem), the cluster of houses on the extreme right.

CAESAREA PHILIPPI

The region at the foot of Mount Hermon near the source of the river Jordan is very beautiful, and from earliest times it was a settlement. Philip, prince of this northern region of Palestine (Luke 3 : 1), built a city on the site of the original settlement and called it Caesarea in honour of the Roman emperor Tiberius Caesar. It was known as Caesarea of Philip, or Caesarea Philippi, to distinguish it from the city of the same name on the coast (**59**). Caesarea Philippi was the scene of Peter's 'confession' (Mark 8 : 27–9).

Infra-red photography makes it possible to take pictures over great distances, and this infra-red photograph (**42**) shows the scenery as one looks north towards Mount Hermon, snow-covered in the far distance in the middle of the skyline, with Caesarea Philippi at its foot. One of the sources of the river Jordan is near Caesarea Philippi (**32**), and here the river begins its tortuous journey from Mount Hermon to the Dead Sea.

**42** *Near Caesarea Philippi: looking towards Mount Hermon in the far distance*

**43** *Old road from Jerusalem to Jericho*

JERICHO

Jericho lies in the Jordan valley 5 miles from the northern end of the Dead Sea and about 20 miles from Jerusalem. The city is 820 feet below sea-level and in consequence has a tropical climate. It was here that Jesus touched the eyes of two blind men, and 'at once their sight came back, and they went on after him' (Matt. 20: 29–34); and here also Zacchaeus, 'superintendent of taxes and very rich', climbed a sycamore-tree (**77**) 'to see what Jesus looked like' (Luke 19: 1–10).

The road 'from Jerusalem down to Jericho' (Luke 10: 30) falls some 3220 feet in a journey of only 21 miles. It twists and turns between limestone crags and bare hills (**43**), and the district lends itself admirably to the activities of highway robbers. The telegraph poles in the picture give a modern touch to the scene, but in ancient times it must have been a dangerous road on which to travel alone. Jesus used it as the setting for a well-known story about a friendly Samaritan (Luke 10: 25–37).

The place known as Jericho has occupied at least three different sites in the same neighbourhood during its long history. The ancient city that Joshua captured (Josh. 6: 1–26) has been rebuilt many times and its position is marked today by the mound seen in the middle distance of this photograph (**44**). The edge of this mound also forms the foreground of the photograph of the Mount of Temptation (**31**). Ancient Jericho has been extensively excavated, in recent years brilliantly by Dr Kathleen Kenyon. The modern village can be seen sprawled round the mound and extending some distance from it. Of the city built by Herod the Great only archaeological traces remain, but they are sufficient to show that it was a magnificent city in Jesus's day.

This picture (**44**) shows the setting of Jericho in the deep valley between the hills on either side of the river Jordan, and the rich fertility of this low-lying area. Jericho was known to the Hebrews as 'the city of palm trees' (Deut. 34: 3).

**44** *Jericho*

**45** *Mount Tabor*

## MOUNT TABOR

Mount Tabor (**45**) is the 'high mountain' traditionally associated with the Transfiguration (Matt. 17: 1–8). It stands 1300 feet above the Plain of Esdraelon, between Nazareth and the Sea of Galilee. In **46** it is seen in the distance across the plain. Jerome, who gave us the Latin translation of the Bible (**124**), described it as having 'a marvellous roundness'. If, as some scholars think, there was a town on the summit of Mount Tabor in Christ's day, it is difficult to understand Matthew's description of it as 'a high mountain where they were alone' (Matt. 17: 1). In view of this difficulty it is sometimes suggested that Mount Hermon in the north of Palestine (**42**) might be the mountain of the Transfiguration.

JERUSALEM

A range of hills, broken only by the Plain of Esdraelon (**46**), runs the full length of Palestine to the west of the Jordan valley (**33**). On a lofty tableland in this range, opposite the northern end of the Dead Sea, a fortified hill-city stood, even before the conquest of Canaan by the Israelites. It was known to the Assyrians as Urusalim, but in the Bible it is variously referred to as Jebus (Josh. 18 : 28), Salem or Zion (Ps. 76 : 2), the city of David (2 Sam. 5 : 7), or Jerusalem (very frequently).

About 1000 B.C. David captured this city and made it his capital (2 Sam. 5 : 6–9). It grew in size and importance, first by the building of Solomon's temple and palaces, then by expansion westward. As a result of these and later building developments the

**46** *Mount Tabor: a distant view across the Plain of Esdraelon*

**47** *Jerusalem: view from the air*

contour of the city has changed; valleys have been filled in and hills have been reduced, but the valleys to the south, east and west of the city have remained unchanged.

The aerial view of Jerusalem from the south (**47**) and the map (**191**) show these features very plainly. The 'Old City' (i.e. the medieval city) is seen within the walls. The Kedron valley flanks the east side of the temple area (recognized by the Dome of the Rock (**49**)), and the Mount of Olives is still farther to the east, in bright sunlight in the photograph. The valley of Hinnom begins in the middle distance to the left of the picture, runs south-west for a short distance, then turns east to join the Kedron valley in the middle foreground of the picture. Modern Jerusalem spreads to the north-west of the Old City.

The valley to the east, 'the Kedron ravine' (John 18: 1), separates the city, 'no farther than a Sabbath day's journey' (Acts 1: 12), from the Mount of Olives. It is seen, palm and olive trees growing in it, in the foreground of this view from the walls of the Old City (**48**). The Mount of Olives is the hill seen in the distance across the valley. It rises in a gentle slope about 250 feet above the level of the temple terrace. Jesus was often there with his disciples (John 18: 1–2). Just before his arrest he went there to pray and Luke says he 'made his way as usual to the Mount of Olives' (Luke 22: 39). Sometimes he would 'leave the city and spend the night on the hill called Olivet' (Luke 21: 37).

The road running across the picture from left to right is the road to Bethany, and eventually to Jericho (**43**). The church on the roadside with a painted fresco over the porch stands on the spot traditionally associated with the agony of Jesus, when 'his sweat was like clots of blood falling to the ground' (Luke 22: 44). In this church there is a jagged piece of rock jutting out of the ground, known as the Rock of Agony. The enclosure immediately to the left of the church is known today as the Garden of Gethsemane but, although the garden must have been somewhere in this area, it is impossible for us to know the exact site of the 'place called Gethsemane' (Matt. 26: 36). The middle tower of the three seen on the hilltop marks the traditional place of the Ascension, although Luke names Bethany as the place where 'in the act of blessing' the disciples, Jesus 'parted from them' (Luke 24: 50–1).

**48** *Jerusalem: Mount of Olives*

**49** *Jerusalem: view of the city from the Mount of Olives*

The view across the Kedron ravine in the opposite direction (**49**) shows the position of the Mount of Olives, from which the photograph has been taken, 'facing the temple' (Mark 13 : 3). The walls of the city and the Golden Gate, now walled-up, are seen in the middle distance, with the Dome of the Rock (a Moslem mosque) on the site of Solomon's temple beyond the walls. It was as Jesus 'approached the descent from the Mount of Olives' (Luke 19 : 37) when he was about to enter Jerusalem riding on a donkey that 'crowds of people carpeted the road with their cloaks, and some cut branches from the trees to spread in his path' (Matt. 21 : 8), and shouted ' "Hosanna! Blessings on him who comes in the name of the Lord! God bless the king of Israel!" ' (John 12 : 13).

**50** *Jerusalem: valley of Hinnom*

The ravine that flanks part of the west boundary of the city and the whole of the south boundary, and joins the Kedron ravine, is the valley of Hinnom (**50**). In the time of Jeremiah, and perhaps earlier, this valley was associated with evil religious practices, even child sacrifice (2 Kings 23 : 10; Jer. 7 : 31). It was still a place with a bad reputation in New Testament times. The valley of Hinnom became the rubbish-tip for the city, and refuse was continually burning there. Its Hebrew name, Ge-Hinnom, became corrupted to Gehenna, and it is this Greek word that is used in the gospels to describe the place of eternal punishment for sin. It is translated 'hell' (Mark 9: 43) or 'the fires of hell' (Matt. 5: 22) in the New English Bible.

In the photograph, the beginning of the valley of Hinnom before it turns eastward is seen diagonally across the middle of the picture. The barbed-wire entanglement in the foreground marks the 'no man's land' that has existed between Israel and Jordan since the division of the land in 1948. The photograph is taken from the Israel side, looking into Jordan. The walls of the Old City are seen across the valley, and the tower in the centre of the picture marks the place where Herod's palace stood.

The extensive building schemes carried out by Herod the Great in Jerusalem included the reconstruction on a lavish scale, and the considerable enlargement, of the ruined temple. Marble and gold were among the materials used and the restored temple was noted for its glittering magnificence. Once when Jesus and his disciples were looking at the temple, one of them was prompted to exclaim: 'Look, Master, what huge stones! What fine buildings!' (Mark 13 : 1). This drawing (**51**), based on the description of the temple given by Josephus and other Jewish writers, gives an impression of the probable appearance of the temple area in the time of Christ. It should be studied with the plan of the temple (**192**).

The great outer court, more than 500 yards long and more than 300 yards wide, was paved with stone slabs and surrounded by massive walls and magnificent covered cloisters.

The south side of the court was the finest. It was known as the Royal Porch and Josephus says it had three aisles and 62 pillars supporting a richly carved wooden ceiling. It may have been here that the dealers and the money-changers conducted their business (John 2 : 14). The covered way on the east side was called Solomon's Cloister. It was here, as 'Jesus was walking in the temple precincts, in Solomon's Cloister', when the 'festival of the Dedication was being held', that 'the Jews picked up stones to stone him' (John 10 : 22–39); and it was here, too, that Peter addressed the crowd, following the healing of 'a man who had been a cripple from birth' who used to be 'laid every day by the gate of the temple called "Beautiful Gate", to beg from people as they went in' (Acts 3 : 1–16).

**51** *Herod's Temple*

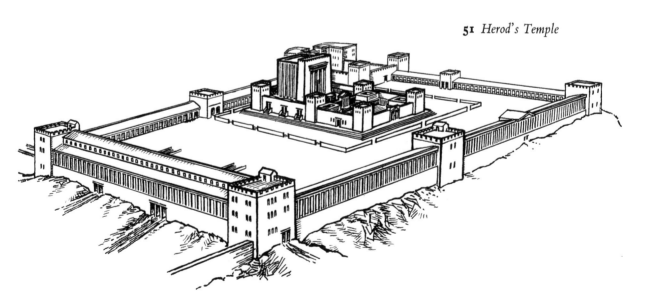

Gentiles were allowed to promenade in this outer court, but they were forbidden to go beyond the balustrade that fenced off the sacred enclosure. The penalty for trespassing was death, and warning notices in Greek were put up at several points. One of these was found in 1871 (**52**). It reads: 'Let no foreigner enter inside the barrier and the fence around the sanctuary. Whosoever is caught will be the cause of death following as a penalty.' Paul may have had this 'dividing wall' in mind when he wrote about 'the enmity' between Jews and Gentiles which Christ's death removed (Eph. 2: 14). In New Testament times the Court of the Gentiles had been turned into 'a thoroughfare for carrying goods' (Mark 11: 16), 'a market' (John 2: 16), and Jesus called it 'a robbers' cave' (Mark 11: 17). When he saw 'the dealers in cattle, sheep, and pigeons, and the money-changers seated at their tables', he 'made a whip of cords and drove them out of the temple, sheep, cattle and all' and 'upset the tables of the money-changers, scattering their coins' (John 2: 13–15).

Beyond the balustrade, the Beautiful Gate led up to the Women's Court, beyond which Jewish women were forbidden to go; and from this court another magnificent gate led up to the Court of Israel into which only male Jewish worshippers were allowed. The Priests' Court surrounded the temple itself, and only priests were allowed inside this enclosure. The temple was 50 yards long, 35 yards wide, and 45 yards high, and it was divided by a curtain into two parts, the sanctuary and the holy place. The gospel writers say that when Jesus on the cross 'breathed his last . . . the curtain of the temple was torn in two from top to bottom' (Matt. 27: 50–1); and the author of Hebrews says that 'the blood of Jesus makes us free to enter boldly into the sanctuary by the new, living way which he has opened for us through the curtain, the way of his flesh' (Heb. 10: 19–20).

In the north-west corner of the temple area Herod built a fortress for defence in time of war (**191**). He named it the Fortress of Antonia to honour Mark Antony, but the New English Bible refers to it as 'the barracks' (Acts 21: 37). On one occasion some 'Jews from the province of Asia' saw Paul in the temple, having previously seen him in the city with Trophimus the Ephesian. They wrongly assumed that Paul had brought this Gentile with him beyond the balustrade, thus profaning the temple. Paul was beaten and arrested, 'the whole crowd . . . yelling "Kill him!"', and then 'taken into the barracks' (Acts 21: 27–40).

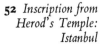

**52** *Inscription from Herod's Temple: Istanbul*

**53** *Jerusalem: Wailing Wall*

Herod's temple was destroyed by the Roman army under Titus, but contrary to his orders, in A.D. 70. A Moslem mosque (the Mosque of Omar, sometimes called the Dome of the Rock) has occupied the site since the seventh century A.D. (**49**). The mosque is the domed building seen in the temple area. Part of the wall built on the west side of the temple area is still standing. This piece of wall was a special place of prayer for Jews until the partition of Israel and Jordan in 1948, since when Jews have been excluded from the temple area. It is known as the Wailing Wall and is so called from the peculiar wailing voice in which Jews in their prayers at the wall lamented the loss of Israel's glory. This photograph (**53**) was evidently taken before 1948. It shows the 'huge stones' (Mark 13 : 1) of which the wall is built, worshippers at prayer facing the wall, and pious Jews leaving the wall after their devotions.

**54** *Jerusalem: the Pavement*

**55** *Jerusalem: a soldiers' game on the Pavement*

The 'Pavement' on which Pilate 'took his seat on the tribunal' at the trial of Jesus (John 19: 13) is not easy to locate. Traditionally it is supposed to have been the court-yard of the Fortress of Antonia ('the barracks') at the north-west corner of the temple area (**191**), and excavations in this region have uncovered a floor made of large stone slabs with a gutter to take the rain water (**54**). This pavement now serves as the floor of the basement in the Convent of the Sisters of Sion. The cloisters built over it are modern. Marks scratched on one of the stone slabs (**55**) are thought to have been used in a game played by the soldiers of the fortress when they were off duty. An alternative suggestion is that the 'Pavement' was the area in front of Herod's palace in the north-west corner of the upper city (**191**).

Bethesda (**56**) is the Hebrew name of the 'place with five colonnades' adjoining 'the Sheep-Pool in Jerusalem' (John 5: 2). The water in this pool was thought to have healing properties, and superstitious stories were told about its powers. Excavations in the north-east area of Jerusalem carried out in 1888 revealed a pool with five porches that may be Bethesda, the scene of the notable miracle of healing described in John 5: 1–9.

**56** *Jerusalem: Pool of Bethesda*

**57** *Jerusalem: Pool of Siloam*

The pool of Siloam (**57**) is another stretch of water in the city of Jerusalem. It is situated in the south of the city and is 58 feet long and 18 feet wide. The tunnel, cut by Hezekiah to ensure an adequate water supply in the city in case of siege (2 Chron. 32: 30), brings water a distance of nearly 600 yards from the spring of Gihon outside the city to the pool of Siloam. A man 'blind from his birth' was told by Jesus to 'wash in the pool of Siloam'. When he obeyed he found he could see (John 9: 1–7).

**58** *Jerusalem: Via Dolorosa*

The Via Dolorosa (i.e. the way of sorrow) is the name given to the route that leads through the Old City (i.e. the medieval city) and which is used by pious pilgrims to represent the way Jesus went from 'the Governor's headquarters' to 'the place called Golgotha' (Mark 15: 16, 22), carrying his cross (**148** and **149**). A thirteenth-century friar was probably the first to make this journey as a pilgrimage. Modern pilgrims cover the route every Friday, halting at each of the fourteen 'stations' of the cross to pray and meditate. This photograph of part of the Via Dolorosa (**58**) gives some idea of the 'traffic problem' that can arise today in this narrow staircase street. The way of the cross that Jesus took is several feet below the present street level of the Old City and only careful expert investigation by archaeologists could tell us if the Via Dolorosa follows the original route.

## CAESAREA

The Mediterranean coastline of Palestine lacks natural harbours. To remedy this defect Herod the Great built an artificial seaport, which he called Caesarea in honour of the Roman emperor Augustus Caesar. Herod also instituted games to be played at Caesarea every five years in honour of Augustus (Josephus: *Antiquities of the Jews*, xv, 8, 1). Again according to Josephus (*Antiquities of the Jews*, xix, 8, 8), it was when Herod Agrippa I, Herod's grandson, was presiding at these games that he met his sudden death (Acts 12: 19–23). It is said to have taken twelve years to build Caesarea. Its harbour had a huge sea mole 200 feet in width. Caesarea was the capital of the Roman province of Judaea and the headquarters of the Roman governors, although it was inconveniently far (about 65 miles by road) from Jerusalem. Cornelius, 'a centurion in the Italian Cohort, as it was called' was stationed there (Acts 10: 1). Caesarea was also 'the home of Philip the evangelist, who was one of the Seven' (Acts 21: 8), and Paul's trial before Felix, Agrippa and Festus, the Roman governor at the time, took place there (Acts 25: 1—26: 32).

The photograph (**59**) shows the fine Roman theatre which has been excavated at Caesarea. The stone slab showing the name of Pontius Pilate (**10**) was discovered here.

**59** *Caesarea: the Roman theatre*

**60** *Megiddo: view of the excavations*

## MEGIDDO

The name Armageddon (Rev. 16: 16) may be derived from Har-Megiddo, which means mountain of Megiddo, and the author of the Revelation may have had this in mind when he made Armageddon the battlefield on which would be fought the final conflict between the nations.

Megiddo was a settlement from very early times, and its position at the meeting-point of busy trade routes made it an important city. Solomon recognized its value in time of war and greatly strengthened it and built there the stables to house his considerable cavalry. Because it commanded the Plain of Esdraelon, an important pass between the mountains west of the Jordan, it was the scene of many battles in Old Testament times (see e.g. Judg. 5: 19–20; 2 Kings 23: 28–30). This photograph (**60**) shows the result of the excavations at Megiddo between 1925 and 1939. A particularly fine Canaanitish altar can be seen near the middle of the picture. The pass through the mountains is in the distance.

# 3 SOCIAL AND RELIGIOUS: LIFE IN NEW TESTAMENT TIMES

## HOUSES

Most of the population in New Testament times lived in single-storey houses. The only room in such houses consisted of two parts, one raised about a yard above the other, with a short flight of steps leading from the lower to the higher. Cattle lived in the lower part of the house; the family in the higher. The roof, made of tree branches and broad leaves covered with a layer of earth, was obviously not very substantial, for the four friends of the paralysed man had no difficulty in breaking through 'over the place where Jesus was' to lower the stretcher on which the sick man was lying (Mark 2: 1–5). In a better-built house the flat roof could be used for strolling ('at eventide . . . David . . . walked upon the roof of the king's house'; 2 Sam. 11: 2), or for prayer ('Peter went up on the roof to pray'; Acts 10: 9). The building of a parapet to prevent accident was enforced by an old law which says 'When thou buildest a new house, then thou shalt make a battlement for thy roof, that thou bring not blood upon thine house, if any man fall from thence' (Deut. 22: 8).

Some of the better-built houses also had 'a room upstairs' (the 'upper room' of the older versions of the New Testament). This was a room on the flat roof that could be reached by an outside staircase. In this picture of Nazareth (**61**) the house in the middle foreground has such a room with two windows. The room in which Jesus ate the 'Passover supper' was 'a large room upstairs' (Mark 14: 12–15), and it was in a similar room that the disciples 'were lodging' after the death and resurrection of Christ (Acts 1: 13).

**61** *Houses in Nazareth*

When Jesus spoke of grass being 'thrown on the stove' (Matt. 6: 30) he had not in mind anything like a modern stove. The 'stove' or oven was an important feature in every home in Palestine in Bible times. It was a primitive arrangement for baking the daily batch of bread. The illustration (**62**) shows an oven in a poor house in Palestine today that is probably not very different from the kind of oven Jesus knew in his own home at Nazareth. This oven is little more than a hole in the thickness of the wall in which a fire can be lit to heat it, and then drawn out when the dough is put in. Sometimes the 'stove' was merely a hole in the ground. Another way of baking bread was to heat an earthenware jar and then to stick thin loaves on the inside of the jar to bake.

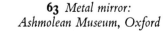

**62** *Primitive oven*                    **63** *Metal mirror: Ashmolean Museum, Oxford*

MIRROR

Paul writes of a mirror in which 'only puzzling reflections' can be seen (1 Cor. 13 : 12). He probably had in mind the kind of mirror illustrated here (**63**). This mirror is a common Roman type, probably to be dated in New Testament times. It is of bronze and part of its polished surface can be seen at the top of the picture. It obviously would not give a very clear reflection. The mirror is shown partly covered by the case which was made to fit neatly over it. A handle by which it could be hung up is fixed to heads of the Egyptian goddess Hathor.

**64** *Ploughing: goad and stony ground*

PLOUGHING

Ploughing was a primitive process in Bible times, as it still is today in some parts of Palestine. A pole made from a branch of a tree had a yoke at one end and a sharpened stick or piece of iron at the other. A simple handle set at right angles to the pole enabled the ploughman to guide his plough by hand (**64**). A man who 'sets his hand to the plough and then keeps looking back' is a poor ploughman (Luke 9: 62).

A long stick sharpened at one end or tipped with an iron point was used to urge forward the animal drawing the plough. It was called a goad, and 'kicking against the goad' (Acts 26: 14) was what only a silly animal would do: the only result was to cause injury to itself. The ploughman in the illustration has a long goad in his left hand and he is controlling the plough with his right.

This picture also shows the sort of stony ground with which farmers in many parts of Palestine have to contend. Jesus told a parable about a sower, some of whose seed 'fell on rocky ground', and he may have had this kind of field in mind (Matt. 13: 4–9).

**65** *Ploughing: yoke*                    **66** *Ploughing: animals unequally yoked*

The two donkeys in this picture (**65**) are dragging the plough and taking the full weight of it by means of the yoke, the wooden pole and its fittings seen resting across the necks of the animals. If the yoke is badly made or carelessly fitted it causes discomfort: if it is skilfully made and carefully fitted it lightens the work of ploughing.

Jesus had this in mind when he spoke of the burden of the law imposed on men by the teaching of the Pharisees, who 'make up heavy packs and pile them on men's shoulders' (Matt. 23 : 4); and compared it with his own teaching, which takes the heavy load of the law from their shoulders. He said: 'Come to me, all whose work is hard, whose load is heavy . . . Bend your necks to my yoke. . . . For my yoke is good to bear, my load is light' (Matt. 11 : 28–30).

Some Palestinian farmers still use a very primitive sort of plough pulled by one animal, but requiring two if the soil is heavy or the field is on a slope. If two animals are needed, a 'yoke of oxen' (Luke 14 : 19) is often used. An Old Testament law says 'Thou shalt not plow with an ox and an ass together' (Deut. 22 : 10), but this law was sometimes overlooked by a poor farmer who could not afford two oxen. This illustration (**66**) shows such a situation, and it is the circumstance Paul had in mind when he wrote: 'Do not unite yourselves with unbelievers; they are no fit mates for you' (2 Cor. 6 : 14). The Greek word used means 'to be yoked with one of another kind'.

## THRESHING

Each grain of wheat is encased in a husk of tough material which would spoil the flour if grain and husk were ground together. The husk must therefore be removed before the corn is ground. A winnowing shovel is then used to toss the mixture of grain and chaff in the air on a windy day, when the light chaff is blown away and the heavier grain falls in a heap on the threshing-floor (**67**).

When John the Baptist preached in the wilderness of Judaea he announced the coming of one 'mightier' than himself and said of him: 'His shovel is ready in his hand and he will winnow his threshing-floor; the wheat he will gather into his granary, but he will burn the chaff on a fire that can never go out' (Matt. 3: 12). John meant that the teaching of the one mightier than himself would separate those who received it from those who rejected it as surely as winnowing separates wheat from chaff.

In primitive communities grain is threshed either by beating it with a stick or by letting an animal trample it or draw a rough sledge over it. In this scene (**68**) at a 'threshing-floor' (Matt. 3: 12) on Mount Carmel, a horse is dragging a sledge over the corn that has recently been cut, and a camel in the background is bringing another load of corn to be threshed. The boy is standing on the sledge to give it extra weight and so make it more effective.

An Old Testament law says: 'Thou shalt not muzzle the ox when he treadeth out the corn' (Deut. 25: 4), and this, if it is obeyed, gives the animal the right to eat some of the food it is helping to produce. In this picture the law is not being obeyed; the horse is prevented from eating the corn on the ground. The New Testament twice quotes this law, which reads in the New English Bible: 'A threshing ox shall not be muzzled' (1 Cor. 9: 9; 1 Tim. 5: 18). The writer had in mind the problem that arose in the Church of his day in connection with the financial support of 'those who labour at preaching and teaching' (1 Tim. 5: 17), himself among them. He uses the case of the threshing ox to show that 'the workman earns his pay' (1 Tim. 5: 17–18) and that he works 'in the hope of getting some of the produce' (1 Cor. 9: 10).

**67** *Winnowing*

**68** *A threshing-floor on Mount Carmel*

**69** *Grinding*

## GRINDING

Grinding was often done by hand in New Testament times and the process was a daily one to ensure a supply of fresh bread every day. The mill consisted of two stones one above the other. The lower stone was heavy and remained stationary; the upper stone was round and had a handle by which it could be turned. Corn was fed through a hole in the middle of the upper stone and ground between the two stones (**69**).

There is a vivid word picture in Matt. 24:41 of 'two women grinding at the mill' at the time 'when the Son of Man comes'. Jesus says 'one will be taken, the other left'. The words are intended to bring home with telling force the meaning of his prediction that 'the Son of Man will come at the time you least expect him' (Matt. 24:44).

## WINEPRESS

When the grape harvest was ready the fruit was gathered in baskets and thrown into a shallow trough dug in the ground. The grapes were then trodden by labourers to squeeze out the juice. In one of his parables Jesus tells of a landowner who planted a vineyard and 'hewed out a winepress' (Matt. 21:33). Treading grapes like this is sometimes used in the Bible as an illustration of 'the great winepress of God's wrath' (Rev. 14:19–20; 19:15). The remains of an ancient winepress are seen in this photograph (**70**). It was found at the traditional birthplace of John the Baptist, and it is hewn out of the rock. The grapes were put in the trough shown in the foreground where the man is standing and the juice ran through holes into another trough dug at a lower level. The winepress in the picture is not in use today: the people are only shown to indicate the size of the press.

**70** *Winepress*

WINE-SKINS

Glass was rare and expensive in New Testament times, and 'bottles' were often made from the skins of animals, cleaned and prepared to hold liquids. After a time skins become dry and brittle, and if 'new wine' is put into 'old wine-skins' it will continue to ferment and may eventually burst the skins 'and then the wine runs out and the skins are spoilt'. Only 'fresh skins' are tough enough and elastic enough to withstand the pressure of the gas from fermenting wine (Matt. 9: 17). The illustration (**71**) shows a water-seller carrying skins such as Jesus referred to in the parable. One of the skins in the photograph is leaking rather badly.

**71** *Wine-skins*

**72** *Fishing: cast net*

**73** *Fishing: draw net*

FISHING

Peter and Andrew were 'casting a net into the lake' when Jesus called them to be his disciples and become 'fishers of men' (Matt. 4: 18–19). The net was circular and had weights round its edge and sometimes a rope attached to its centre. Similar nets are occasionally seen in use in Palestine today (**72**). The fisherman wades into the shallow water and throws the net into deeper water. The weights cause the net to open and fall flat on the surface of the water when it is thrown, and to close to form a bag as it falls through the water. The net and any fish it may have enclosed are then pulled to the shore by means of the rope.

James and John were 'overhauling their nets' when Jesus called them to be his disciples (Matt. 4: 21–2), but their nets were different from the one described above, and different Greek words are used in the gospels for the two kinds of nets. The nets used by James and John were in long lengths, having floats at the top and weights at the bottom. It was necessary to 'shoot' this kind of net from a boat (John 21: 3), or boats (Luke 5: 7), and to leave it hanging in the water for some time before hauling it in (**73**). The net mentioned by Jesus in one of his parables (Matt. 13: 47–8) which had to be 'let down into the sea' and then 'dragged ashore' sounds like a simple form of the trawl net with which we are familiar today.

**74** *Olive press*

MILLSTONE

When olives are squeezed, olive oil is forced out of them. An oil press is used in the first part of this process (**74**). It consists of two parts: a round stone trough into which the olives are put, and a heavy millstone which can be rolled round on its edge inside the trough. A wooden shaft (not shown in this illustration) is fitted to the millstone and a donkey yoked to it rolls the stone by walking round in a circle. It was this kind of millstone that Jesus had in mind when he said it would be better for a man 'to have a millstone hung round his neck and be drowned in the depths of the sea' than for him to be 'a cause of stumbling' to 'little ones' who have faith (Matt. 18: 6). The Greek word used means literally 'a donkey millstone'.

SHEPHERDS

Shepherds in Palestine neither drive their sheep nor use sheepdogs. Instead, a 'good shepherd' is one who 'calls his own sheep by name, and leads them out'. As this illustration (**75**) shows, 'he goes ahead and the sheep follow, because they know his voice'. Jesus once reminded his hearers of the way of a shepherd with his sheep, and then described himself as 'the good shepherd' (John 10: 1–18).

A flock of sheep and goats grazing together is a common sight in Palestine today (**76**) as it must have been in the time of Christ. The hill in the background of this picture is the Mount of Temptation (**31**). In one of his parables Jesus speaks of a shepherd who 'separates the sheep from the goats', and compares him with 'the Son of Man ... in his glory ... in state on his throne, with all the nations gathered before him' who will similarly 'separate men into two groups'. To the group who have helped those in distress and so helped him, Christ will give the 'Father's blessing': to those who have not, he will bring punishment, dispatching them 'to the eternal fire that is ready for the devil and his angels' (Matt. 25 : 31–46).

**75** *Shepherd leading sheep*

**76** *Sheep and goats at foot of Mount of Temptation*

**77** *Sycamore-tree*

SYCAMORE-TREE

The 'sycamore-tree' that Zacchaeus climbed because 'he was eager to see what Jesus looked like' (Luke 19:3) was not the tree to which we give that name today. It was a broad-leaved tree that bore clusters of a sweet fruit something like a fig. The illustration (**77**) shows the unusually wide spread of its branches, a quality that makes it specially suitable for planting along the roadside to provide shade in a hot country like Palestine.

**78** *Passover table:*
*Muswell Hill, London*

## PASSOVER

Three celebrations of the annual festival of Passover are mentioned by John during the ministry of Jesus (John 2: 13; 6: 4; 11: 55). The synoptic gospels reckon the Last Supper as a celebration of the festival (**200**). At the 'Passover supper' (Matt. 26: 17) in addition to unleavened bread (i.e. bread made without yeast), a roasted lamb and bitter herbs, symbolizing the bitter experience of the Israelites in Egypt, were eaten, and wine was drunk. In more recent times other symbolic foods have been added to the Passover menu and other customs have been included in the ceremonial meal. The photographs show a Passover table set in a London school for Jewish children (**78**), and a nomadic Jewish family now settled in Palestine eating their first Passover there (**79**). In both pictures the service books, the thin round discs of unleavened bread, and the wine are clearly seen.

**79** *Passover table: Israel*

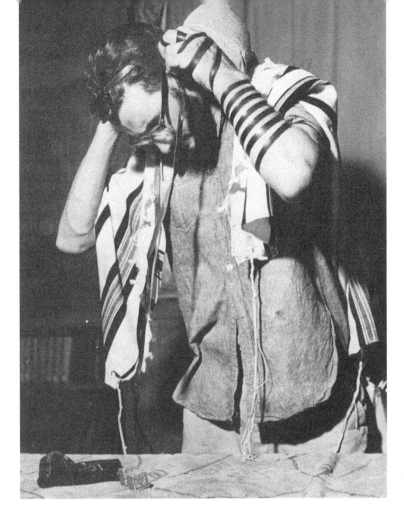

**80** *Phylacteries and tallit*

## FRINGES

The law instructs Jews to wear 'fringes in the borders of their garments' (Num. 15 : 38), and in New Testament times this law was obeyed by wearing a scarf or shawl with tassels (called 'fringes' in the New English Bible) as part of the normal dress. Jesus accused 'the doctors of the law and the Pharisees' of wearing 'deep fringes on their robes' for show (Matt. 23 : 5).

Nowadays this scarf is only worn at the times of prayer. It is called a tallit and it has tassels at the corners, each of which consists of eight strands tied in five knots. Some Jews read a meaning into these numbers. Each Hebrew letter has a corresponding number, and when the numbers of the letters in the Hebrew word for fringes are added together, the total is 600. This 600 added to 8 (the number of strands) and 5 (the number of knots) comes to 613, the number of commands the scribes have counted in the Old Testament books of the law. The illustration (**80**) shows how the tallit is worn. The eight strands and the five knots can be counted on one of the tassels in the picture. The stripes across the ends of the tallit have no special significance.

PHYLACTERIES

In its original form a phylactery (Greek for an 'amulet' or a 'charm') was a strip of parchment on which four passages from the Old Testament were written in Hebrew. The passages are Exod. 13 : 1–10; Exod. 13 : 11–16; Deut. 6 : 4–9; Deut. 11 : 13–21. A phylactery of the time of Jesus was recently found in a cave 12 miles to the south of Qumran. Three of the four passages are written on this strip, and a smaller fragment of parchment was found near it on which the fourth passage was written. The law about phylacteries is this: 'Thou shalt bind them for a sign upon thine hand, and they shall be for frontlets between thine eyes' (Deut. 6 : 8). Some Jews take this law literally, wearing phylacteries on the forehead and the left arm and hand at the times of prayer. Jesus accused 'the doctors of the law and the Pharisees' of wearing 'broad phylacteries' (Matt. 23 : 5), which means, presumably, that they wore outrageously large pieces of parchment for show.

**81** *Phylacteries being made*

**82** *Phylactery scroll*

In more recent times the parchment strips have been enclosed in small leather boxes painted black and fastened to a leather base to which long leather thongs are attached. One of these boxes is worn on the forehead, the leather thongs passing round the head and then falling over the shoulders to the front of the body; and the other is worn on the left upper arm, the leather thong being bound seven times round the forearm and tied round the hand in such a way as to form the Hebrew letter *shin*, the initial letter of one of the Hebrew names for God. All this is intended to remind the worshipper that it is the perfect God (seven is the 'perfect' number, perhaps because it was once believed that sun and moon and the five planets formed a perfect group of heavenly bodies) who must be worshipped with the whole heart (the arm phylactery is near the heart when the arm is folded across the body) and with the whole mind (the head phylactery is near the brain, which today is assumed to be associated with the mind).

In the illustration (**80**) a Jew is seen putting on his phylacteries, and the features mentioned above are plainly visible (the letter *shin* is something like our letter W, but in this position of the man's hand it is upside-down). On the table are the cardboard covers and the velvet bag in which the phylacteries are kept when not in use.

This illustration (**81**) shows phylacteries being made. On the extreme right a half-made head phylactery is seen. It has four divisions to receive four pieces of parchment with one passage written on each. The four passages mentioned above are on one piece of parchment in the arm phylactery. Phylacteries that are complete except for the fitting of the thongs, and others in various stages of manufacture, are to be seen on the bench in the foreground.

The second of the four passages (Exod. 13 : 11–16) from a modern head phylactery is shown here in actual size (**82**). It is larger than usual, somewhat like the 'broad phylacteries' referred to above. The scribe who copied this passage has added fine strokes above some of the letters, a form of decoration known as 'crowning'.

**83** *Synagogue: Bevis Marks, London*

## SYNAGOGUE

A synagogue (Greek for 'a bringing together') is a Jewish place of worship. In New Testament times synagogues were built wherever there was a community of Jews: e.g. Salamis in Cyprus (Acts 13 : 5), Pisidian Antioch (Acts 13 : 14–15), Iconium (Acts 14 : 1), as well as, of course, Jerusalem and many other places in Palestine. Jesus worshipped 'regularly' (Luke 4 : 16) in the synagogue, and at one stage in his ministry 'he went round the whole of Galilee, teaching in the synagogues' (Matt. 4 : 23). Paul and Barnabas, similarly, 'on the Sabbath . . . went to synagogue and took their seats' (Acts 13 : 14).

**84** *Synagogue: King George Avenue, Jerusalem*

A synagogue is usually a plain building, but the ark, a cupboard in which the scrolls of the law are kept, is often elaborately decorated. Two synagogues are shown here: the synagogue in Bevis Marks, London, opened in 1701 (**83**), and the modern Jeshurun Synagogue in King George Avenue, Jerusalem (**84**). In the photograph of the Bevis Marks Synagogue the ark is open and the scrolls of the law with their richly embroidered mantles and their silver ornaments can easily be seen. The two tablets seen above the ark in both these synagogues, but seen more plainly over the ark in the Bevis Marks Synagogue, have the opening words in Hebrew of each of the ten commandments written on them. The young Jews swarming round the ark in the Jeshurun Synagogue are presumably waiting for the ark to be opened.

Jesus said that 'the doctors of the law and the Pharisees . . . like to have . . . the chief seats in synagogues' (Matt. 23 : 1–6). These 'chief seats' were near the ark, usually facing the congregation.

The Sabbath morning service is mainly occupied with the reading of the law and the prophets. The law is read from sheepskin scrolls on which learned and expert scribes have very carefully copied the books of Genesis, Exodus, Leviticus, Numbers and Deuteronomy (**85**). The Jewish tradition is that Moses wrote these books, variously

**85** *Scribes copying the law*

**86** *Scroll of Isaiah from Qumran: Shrine of the Book, Hebrew University of Jerusalem*

called the law of Moses, the Pentateuch (Greek for 'five books'), or the Torah (Hebrew for 'instruction'), and this is why James said that 'Moses . . . is read in the synagogues Sabbath by Sabbath' (Acts 15: 21). Laymen are called up to the reading-desk to read passages from the law and the prophets, and Jesus was once called up for this purpose in the synagogue at Nazareth. He 'was handed the scroll of the prophet Isaiah', probably like the one found at Qumran (**30**) and shown here open at Isaiah 40 (**86**). He 'opened the scroll', read a passage from Chapter 61, then 'rolled up the scroll, gave it back to the attendant, and sat down'. After the reading he commented on the passage he had read (Luke 4: 16–20). Luke's description of this incident gives us a useful picture of the procedure during a synagogue service, but in addition to the reading there is also the singing of hymns and psalms, and the saying of many prayers.

In English synagogues the tallit (**80**) is worn by the men in the congregation, but in Israel today this is not always the case (**84**). The head is always covered during the service. In orthodox synagogues women and girls sit apart from the men and boys, sometimes in a gallery screened off by a metal grid. A bit of this screen can be seen on the extreme left of the photograph of the Bevis Marks Synagogue (**83**).

REJOICING IN THE LAW

Jews regard the first five books of the Old Testament as the law of Moses, and passages from this part of the Bible must be read in every synagogue in the world every sabbath day (Acts 13 : 15; 15 : 21) in such a way as to ensure that the whole of it is read once a year. To mark the end of one year's reading and the beginning of another there is a parade of the scroll of the law round the synagogue and much rejoicing by the congregation (**87**). At Djerba, an island off the east coast of Tunisia in the Mediterranean, there is one of the oldest synagogues in the world, and this picture shows the scroll in a portable ark being carried round the Djerba synagogue on the occasion of the Rejoicing in the Law. The scroll is open at the beginning of Genesis (remember that Hebrew reads from right to left) where the new cycle of readings is about to begin. The men taking part in the procession are wearing the tallit (**80**), another reminder of the importance of the law in their religious life.

Jews and Christians have different attitudes toward the law, and the New Testament has a good deal to say about this difference. Both Jews and Christians accept Paul's verdict that 'the law is in itself holy, and the commandment is holy and just and good' (Rom. 7: 12), but Christians also believe, and Jews do not believe, the words Paul wrote to the Galatians: 'Thus the law was a kind of tutor in charge of us until Christ should come, when we should be justified through faith; and now that faith has come, the tutor's charge is at an end' (Gal. 3 : 24–5).

**87** *Synagogue at Djerba: Rejoicing in the Law*

*'a letter'* ↓        *'a stroke'*

בְּרֵאשִׁ֛ית

**88** *Jot and tittle*

JOT AND TITTLE

Jesus once said to his disciples: 'I tell you this: so long as heaven and earth endure, not a letter, not a stroke, will disappear from the Law until all that must happen has happened' (Matt. 5: 18). The 'letter' to which Christ referred is the *yod*, the smallest letter in the Hebrew alphabet, and the 'stroke' is the tittle, the small projection on some Hebrew letters (**88**). The same passage in the Authorized and Revised Versions refers to 'one jot or one tittle'.

CHAIR OF MOSES

This stone chair (**89**), of which the high back is missing, was found in the ruins of the synagogue at Chorazin (**38**). It may well be an example of the 'chair of Moses' to which Jesus referred when he said: 'The doctors of the law and the Pharisees sit in the chair of Moses; therefore do what they tell you' (Matt. 23: 2). It is evident from this quotation that the 'chair of Moses' was the special seat of honour reserved in the synagogues for teachers of the law or for distinguished visitors.

The Greek word used for 'chair' is *kathedra*, and it is from this word that we derive our word 'cathedral', because a cathedral contains the bishop's 'chair' or throne.

The inscription on the front of the seat in the illustration commemorates the gift to the synagogue of certain parts of the building, the portico and the steps of the entrance.

**89** *Chair of Moses, from the synagogue at Chorazin*

**90** *Samaritans in the synagogue at Nablus*

SAMARITANS

The Samaritans were a religious group living in Samaria, the region between Galilee and Judaea, in New Testament times. Their origin is obscure, as is the exact cause of the enmity between Jews and Samaritans hinted at by the author of the fourth gospel: 'Jews and Samaritans, it should be noted, do not use vessels in common' (John 4: 9).

A small group of about 120 Samaritans live at Nablus at the foot of Mount Gerizim (**41**). This picture shows some of them at worship in their synagogue there (**90**). They possess a greatly treasured copy of the first five books of the Old Testament, the only part of the Bible they accept. It is probably under the cover on the chair in the middle foreground of the illustration. These Samaritans at Nablus still celebrate the Passover each year on the summit of Mount Gerizim, slaughtering a lamb and living in tents on the hilltop during the week of the festival.

**91** *High priest wearing breastplate*

### BREASTPLATE

The high priest was the supreme representative before God of the Jewish people. The author of the Letter to Hebrews compares the office of the Jewish high priest with the office of Christ, 'a great high priest who has passed through the heavens' (Heb. 4 : 14), and reaches this conclusion: 'The high priests made by the Law are men in all their frailty; but the priest appointed by the words of the oath which supersedes the Law is the Son, made perfect now for ever' (Heb. 7 : 28).

A breastplate was part of the official dress of the Jewish high priest. It consisted of a square of gold in which were set four rows of three precious stones, different in colour, on each of which was inscribed in Hebrew the name of one of the twelve tribes of Israel (Exod. 28 : 15–21) (**91**). In this picture the top row of stones is hidden.

In the New Testament the breastplate is also part of 'the armour which God provides' to help the Christian in his warfare against evil (Eph. 6: 11). For example, in Eph. 6: 14 the breastplate is the symbol for 'integrity' (the word breastplate is translated 'coat of mail'), and in 1 Thess. 5: 8 it is the symbol for 'faith and love'.

In one of the visions described in the Revelation John saw locusts which 'wore breastplates like iron' (Rev. 9: 9), and in another vision horses which 'wore breastplates, fiery red, blue, and sulphur-yellow' (Rev. 9: 17).

### TOMB AND ROUND STONE

In the days when valuables were more often buried with a dead body than they are today, robbing graves was a common crime. Cavelike tombs were 'cut out of the rock' (Matt. 27: 60) and to protect them from thieves a round stone was rolled across the entrance in a groove sloping slightly downwards. It therefore needed considerable strength to roll the stone back against the pull of gravity and to wedge it 'open'. Three women did not expect to be able to manage it when they came to the place where Jesus was buried, although they had come with the express intention of entering the tomb (Mark 16: 1–3).

The illustration (**92**) shows a typical tomb of the time of Jesus with the stone rolled back.

**92** *Tomb and round stone, near Jerusalem*

FESTIVAL OF THE DEDICATION

An eight-branched candlestick (**93**) is used by Jews at one of their festivals, the one called in the New English Bible 'the festival of the Dedication' (John 10: 22). Modern Jews use the Hebrew word for 'dedication' and call it the festival of Hanukkah. It usually falls at Christmastime, and the fourth gospel says 'it was winter' when it was celebrated.

This festival reminds Jews of a story about one of their national heroes, Judas Macca-baeus, told in the Apocrypha (1 Macc. 4: 36–59), and of a legend told about it by their rabbis; namely, that one day's supply of oil burned miraculously in the golden lamps

**93** *Hanukkah candlestick*

**94** *Hanukkah oil lamp, dated 1650: exhibited at Bayswater Synagogue Exhibition, London, 1961*

of the temple at Jerusalem for eight days and nights on the occasion described in the story. The festival therefore lasts eight days, and candles are lit in number corresponding to the day of the festival.

In the illustration a member of a youth organization in a children's village in Israel is lighting the candles on the eighth day of the festival. In order to come a little nearer to the original legend some Jews use, instead of a candlestick, a device containing eight little oil lamps (**94**).

A *seven*-branched candlestick is the symbol of the modern state of Israel. A golden candlestick of this kind was used in the tabernacle (Exod. 25 : 31-7), and later in Herod's temple (**8**).

COINS

The simplest way of conducting business is by barter, and it was by this means that business transactions were carried out in early times. Later, however, bits of precious or semi-precious metals were used as the medium of exchange. Amos noticed that the dishonest traders of his day cheated by making heavy the shekel weights with which they weighed out the customers' bits of metal (Amos 8 : 5). In the seventh century B.C. the Greeks issued shaped pieces of metal with stamped impressions on them, and thus began the use of money as we know it today.

The impressions on coins can sometimes help our understanding of history. Such impressions may include contemporary or near-contemporary portraits of the rulers of the time in which the coins were made, as well as inscriptions in writing and various symbolic representations, all of which may add something to our knowledge of the period.

Money is mentioned fairly frequently in the Bible, but we cannot always be quite sure which coin is referred to. Several coins, some of them mentioned in the New Testament, and others of interest to students of the period, are illustrated in actual size (**95–108**).

**95.** Jews from the age of twenty paid an annual temple-tax towards the upkeep of the temple at Jerusalem, and this silver didrachm (i.e. two drachms) minted at Tyre in 12/11 B.C. was the sort of coin used. Money-changers sat in the temple ready to change worshippers' money into this acceptable kind from Tyre, and on one occasion Jesus 'upset the tables of the money-changers' because, he said, they were making the temple 'a robbers' cave' (Mark 11 : 15–17).

**96.** The 'silver coin' that was sufficient to pay the temple-tax for both Peter and Jesus (Matt. 17: 27), and the 'thirty silver pieces' paid to Judas (Matt. 26: 15) were probably like this silver tetradrachm (i.e. four drachms) minted at Tyre in 80/79 B.C.

**97.** The 'two tiny coins' the poor widow put in the chest in the temple treasury (Mark 12: 42) may have been like this bronze coin minted in the time of Herod the Great. An anchor is represented on one side of the coin.

**98.** Antioch in Syria minted money during the reign of Augustus (**3**) whose portrait is seen on one side of this coin. The letters SC on the other side stand for *Senatus consulto* (i.e. 'by decree of the Senate'). This may be the 'penny' which would buy two sparrows (Matt. 10: 29; they are 'five for twopence' in Luke 12: 6).

**99.** The head of Tiberius (**4**) is seen on this silver coin, and the inscription gives the emperor's titles. It was probably a 'silver piece' like this which was produced at Jesus's request and about which he asked the 'Pharisees and men of Herod's party' who were trying to trap him, 'Whose head is this, and whose inscription?'. Their reply was 'Caesar's' (Mark 12: 13–17).

**95** *Silver didrachm*

**96** *Silver tetradrachm*

**97** *Small coin of the time of Herod the Great*

**99** *Silver piece: Tiberius*

**98** *Coin of Antioch: Augustus*

**100** *Coin of Alexandria: Tiberius and Augustus*

**101** *Small coin of the time of Pontius Pilate*

**103** *Silver coin of Rome: Claudius*

**102** *Bronze coin of Antioch: Tiberius*

**104** *Silver didrachm: Nero*

**105** *Bronze coin of Rome: Nero*

**106** *Bronze coin of Rome: Vespasian*

**107** *Bronze quadrans*

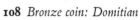

**108** *Bronze coin: Domitian*

**100.** This base-metal coin minted at Alexandria in A.D. 28/29 shows the head of Tiberius (**4**) on one side and on the other side the head of Augustus (**3**) shown as a god wearing a crown with radiating rays. This may have been the coin referred to in Mark 12: 13–17.

**101.** Coins were minted in Roman Palestine during the rule of Pontius Pilate, and this is a bronze coin of that period. The name of Tiberius (**4**) in Greek letters is on one side and the date (*IH*, i.e. the eighteenth year of Tiberius's reign, A.D. 31/32) surrounded by a wreath is on the other side. This may be one of the 'tiny coins' referred to in Mark 12: 42 (cf. **97**).

**102.** The head of Tiberius (**4**) is portrayed on this bronze coin of Antioch. For the meaning of the letters SC, see **98** above.

**103.** This silver coin was minted at Rome in A.D. 46/47 to celebrate the victory of Claudius in Britain. It shows the head of Claudius (**5**) on one side, and on the other side the words *de Britann(is)* on a triumphal arch can be seen.

**104.** Gifts for the poor of Jerusalem may have been brought from Asia by Paul in this kind of money (Acts 24: 17). The coin illustrated is a silver didrachm of Ephesus minted in the time of Nero (**6**) whose portrait is depicted on one side. The word *didrachmon* (the Greek form of didrachm) can be read on the other side.

**105.** This fine bronze coin minted in Rome shows the head of Nero (**6**) surrounded by his titles on one side, and 'Roma' enthroned and holding the symbol of victory on the other side.

**106.** The head of Vespasian (p. 16) appears on one side of this bronze coin minted at Rome in A.D. 71. Vespasian's son, Titus (**7**) destroyed Jerusalem in A.D. 70, and the inscription on the other side reads, *Judaea capta* (i.e. Judaea captured), and shows 'Judaea' sitting in dejection after her defeat.

**107.** The Roman victory in Judaea in A.D. 70 was marked by the minting of the bronze quadrans (i.e. a fourth part) of which this is an example. It bears the impression of a palm-tree as a symbol of victory. The Greek word for 'farthing' in Matt. 5: 26 and Mark 12: 42 is *kodrantes* (i.e. quadrans), but this quadrans was not in circulation in the period of the gospels. The 'farthing' may have been a coin like the one illustrated here.

**108.** This small bronze coin depicting the head of Domitian (**9**) was discovered in a Roman ship embedded in the Thames mud near Blackfriars Bridge in 1962. It was the custom to put a coin under the heel of the mast when a ship was being built, perhaps as an offering to the gods in the hope that they would send good winds. This coin was found in that position.

# The Growth of the
# New Testament

# 1 MANUSCRIPTS IN GREEK

## PAPYRUS

Papyrus is one of the materials on which the books of the New Testament were originally written. It is a thin paper-like substance made from the papyrus plant which grows plentifully on the banks of rivers in warm countries (**109**).

Pith taken from the stalks of the plant was cut into thin strips and these were laid side by side. Other similar strips were laid above and at right angles to them. Glue or the natural juices of the plant held the layers together and pressure between heavy stones compressed them. The surface was made smooth by gentle rubbing. The sheets of papyrus thus made could be joined together to make a long roll, or folded to make the pages of a book. From the early second century, and perhaps before that, New Testament writers used the book (or codex) form rather than the roll or scroll form.

Moisture is the greatest enemy of papyrus, but even if it is kept dry it becomes brittle and fragile with age (see, for example, **113**). The conditions in the Near East are ideal for its preservation, and that is why so many New Testament manuscripts have been found there.

**109** *Papyrus plant*

THE RYLANDS FRAGMENT

This fragment (**110**) of papyrus is the oldest bit of the New Testament known to exist. It is quite small, about $3\frac{1}{2}'' \times 2\frac{1}{2}''$, and it has writing on both sides, evidence that it once belonged to a copy of a gospel in codex form (i.e. book form) rather than scroll form. The side shown on the left of the picture contains parts of John 18: 31–3 and the side shown on the right contains parts of John 18: 37–8. Another illustration (**111**) shows where the fragment (represented by the shaded part) fits in the complete text.

This fragment was found in Egypt in 1920 and is now in the John Rylands Library, Manchester. The gospel of John was probably written towards the end of the first century and the Rylands fragment is thought to have been written in the first half of the second century, very probably about A.D. 150, that is, only about one generation after the original gospel.

**110** *Papyrus fragment: John Rylands Library, Manchester, England*

**111** *Rylands fragment in its context*

εἶπον αὐτῷ οἱ Ἰουδαῖοι Ἡμῖν οὐκ ἔξεστιν
ἀποκτεῖναι οὐδένα· ἵνα ὁ λόγος τοῦ Ἰησοῦ
πληρωθῇ ὃν εἶπεν σημαίνων ποίῳ θανάτῳ
ἤμελλεν ἀποθνήσκειν· Εἰσῆλθεν οὖν πάλιν
εἰς τὸ πραιτώριον ὁ Πειλᾶτος καὶ ἐφώνησ-
εν τὸν Ἰησοῦν καὶ εἶπεν αὐτῷ Σὺ εἶ ὁ βα-
σιλεὺς τῶν Ἰουδαίων;

**112** *Papyrus scroll with seal: Staatliche Museum, Berlin*

## SEALED SCROLL

This scroll (**112**) is one of several found at Elephantine in Egypt. It may be as early as the fifth century B.C. The scroll is folded and sealed, perhaps in outward appearance very much like Paul's letters that were sent to the churches. When John looked through the 'door opened in heaven' (Rev. 4: 1) he 'saw in the right hand of the One who sat on the throne a scroll . . . sealed up with seven seals' (Rev. 5: 1). The illustration shows a similar scroll sealed with one seal. A scroll with seven seals from the early second century was recently discovered in a cave near the Dead Sea.

## UNKNOWN GOSPEL

Luke says: 'Many writers have undertaken to draw up an account of the events that have happened among us, following the traditions handed down to us by the original eyewitnesses' (Luke 1: 1), and John says: 'There is much else that Jesus did. If it were all to be recorded in detail, I suppose the whole world would not hold the books that would be written' (John 21: 25). The illustration (**113**) is of an 'unknown' gospel, perhaps a work of one of the 'many writers' who wrote down some of the 'much else that Jesus did' mentioned in the passage quoted above.

**113** *Fragment of an unknown gospel: British Museum, London*

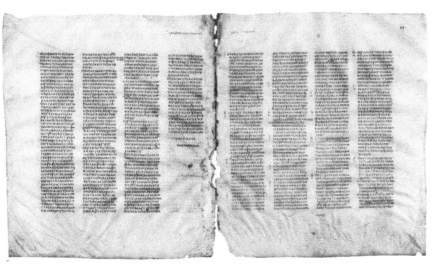

**114** *Codex Sinaiticus: British Museum, London*          **115** *Codex Sinaiticus: the Lord's Prayer*

## THE CODEX SINAITICUS

The Codex Sinaiticus (so called because it was found in a monastery on Mount Sinai) is one of the greatest treasures in the British Museum. It was bought from the Soviet Government in 1933 for £100,000. Written in the fourth century on vellum, it contains the whole of the New Testament (together with the *Epistle of Barnabas* and the *Shepherd of Hermas*, two books not found in our New Testament today) and a good deal of the Old Testament. Vellum made from the skin of a calf, and parchment made from the skins of sheep, goats, deer, and occasionally other animals, became the common substances used in making the best books in the first half of the fourth century. The pages of the Codex Sinaiticus are 15″ × 13½″ and there are four columns to the page, except in the poetical books of the Old Testament where there are only two. It is written on the 'hair' side of the vellum (the side on which the hair grew; the other side is called the 'flesh' side) in large clear Greek capitals (uncials), and there is no separation of the words and very little punctuation. A sharp-pointed instrument has been used to rule lines on the flesh side of the vellum to help the writer.

In the illustration (**114**) the Codex Sinaiticus is shown open at the end of Luke (on the page on the left) and the beginning of John (on the page on the right). The features mentioned above can be seen in this photograph. A second illustration (**115**) shows the text in more detail. The top line of the first column is part of Matt. 6 : 4, and Matthew's version of the Lord's Prayer begins on the eighth line from the bottom of the same column. A third illustration (**116**) shows how later scribes have made corrections to the text and even added passages in the margin which they thought ought to have been included in the first place. A short curly line (e.g. in the 24th line from the top of the first column) is used to show where they think the insertion should be made, and a line of dots (e.g. in the 17th line from the top of the first column) indicates a part of the text that in the opinion of the corrector ought to be omitted.

**116** *Codex Sinaiticus: corrections and additions*

**117** *Codex Alexandrinus: British Museum, London*

## THE CODEX ALEXANDRINUS

The Codex Alexandrinus (so called because it came from Alexandria in Egypt) is in the British Museum. It was written in the first half of the fifth century and contains almost the whole Bible. It came into the possession of Charles I in 1627 and remained in the Royal Library until it was presented to the nation by George II. The pages of the Codex Alexandrinus are $12\frac{3}{4}'' \times 10\frac{1}{4}''$ and there are two columns to a page (**117**). It is written in large round Greek letters.

CODEX VATICANUS

As its name implies, the Codex Vaticanus (**118**) is in the Vatican Library, Rome. It was written at about the same time as the Codex Sinaiticus, i.e. fourth century A.D., and it is usually regarded as the best and the most valuable manuscript of the Greek Bible in our possession. Parts of the New Testament are missing. The pages of the Codex Vaticanus are $10\frac{1}{2}'' \times 10''$, and there are three columns to the page. It is written in rather small delicate Greek capitals, but the writing has been spoiled by a well-meaning scribe who has inked over all the passages he considered to be authentic. An example of this is seen in the illustration. The four lines beginning at the 10th line from the bottom of the middle column have not been retouched because they have been written again by mistake in the original.

**118** *Codex Vaticanus: Vatican, Rome*

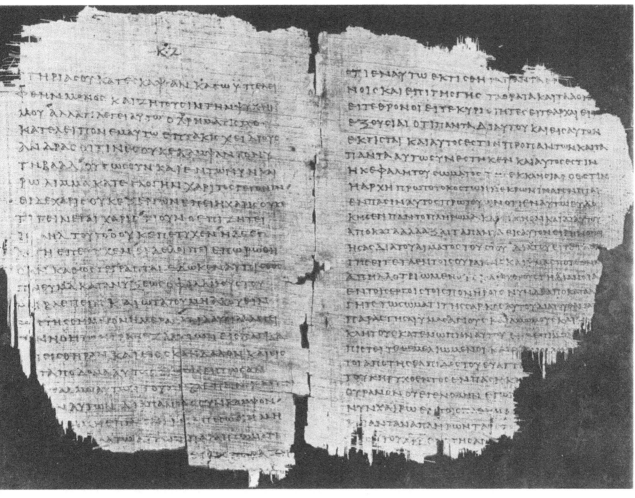

**119** *Chester Beatty manuscript: Chester Beatty Library, Dublin*

## CHESTER BEATTY MANUSCRIPT

About 1930 Mr A. Chester Beatty, an American collector of manuscripts, bought from a dealer in Egypt a number of papyrus leaves from various books of the Greek Bible. Among them were several from the New Testament. This illustration of one of them (**119**), open at Romans 11 : 3–12, shows that they once belonged to a codex (i.e. a book, not a scroll), that the pages were broad and that a single column was written on each page. The writing is small, thus exposing a considerable amount of text at each opening of the codex, and the style is that of the third century A.D., a century or so earlier than the Codex Sinaiticus (**114**). The Chester Beatty collection of manuscripts is now in Dublin.

**120** *Minuscule Greek: British Museum, London*

## MINUSCULE

The Codex Sinaiticus (**114**), the Codex Alexandrinus (**117**) and the Codex Vaticanus (**118**) are written in capital letters, known as uncials. The word probably meant 'inch-high' originally. Uncials make the script easy to read, but they take up a good deal of room. Round about the ninth century A.D. a beautiful style of writing called minuscule (i.e. small letters) or cursive (i.e. a flowing style with letters joined together) was brought into use, and in the tenth century uncial writing generally gave way to minuscule in the best manuscripts. The illustration (**120**) shows a good example of minuscule.

## PALIMPSEST

At a time when vellum was scarce or expensive a scribe might take a 'valueless' manuscript and wash or scrape off as much of the writing as possible (not always very much) and use the vellum again for his own writing. Such a document is called a palimpsest (from two Greek words: *palin*, again; *psao*, to rub smooth). The illustration (**121**) shows a palimpsest now in the British Museum. It is the Codex Nitriensis, so called because it was brought from the Nitrian Desert in Egypt. The partly erased text is a valuable copy of part of Luke's gospel, written in a fine bold hand, probably of the sixth century; whilst the later writing (at right angles to the original text) is a work of Severus of Antioch written in Syriac in the eighth or ninth century.

**121** *Palimpsest: British Museum, London*

### A SYRIAC VERSION

When Christianity spread beyond the borders of Palestine there soon arose the need for translations of the Bible. Syria was nearest northern neighbour to Palestine and translations into Syriac, the language of Syria and Mesopotamia, must have been among the earliest to be made. The best versions we possess in this language are of the fifth century, and one such version is illustrated here (**122**). Syriac reads from right to left, like Hebrew and Arabic.

### A COPTIC VERSION

There was a large colony of Jews in Alexandria in Egypt, and many of them became converts to the Christian faith. Apollos, 'an Alexandrian by birth', was such a one. He 'knew only John's baptism', and he became 'an eloquent man, powerful in his use of the scriptures . . . full of spiritual fervour' (Acts 18: 24–6). Coptic was the language of the Egyptians at that time, and it is the language used in the services of the Church in Egypt today. It was necessary to prepare a copy of the New Testament in Coptic for the use of Egyptian Christians as soon as possible, and a version was actually produced before the end of the second century. Coptic is written in Greek letters. A page from an early Coptic version of the New Testament is illustrated here (**123**).

The *Gospel according to Thomas*, discovered with a number of other apocryphal works near Nag Hammadi, Upper Egypt, in 1946 and now in Cairo, is in Coptic.

**122** *Syriac version: British Museum, London*    **123** *Coptic version: British Museum, London*

**124** *Lindisfarne Gospel: British Museum, London*

## THE LINDISFARNE GOSPELS

The Lindisfarne Gospels are bound in a famous volume now in the British Museum. The text is that of the Latin Vulgate of St Jerome and the book was written by Eadfrith, Bishop of Lindisfarne and Northumbria, who died in A.D. 687. The letters are large and the richly coloured ornamentation at the beginning of each gospel is truly magnificent. The illustration (**124**) shows the beginning of the narrative portion of Matthew's gospel (Matt. 1 : 18).

It is not, however, the Latin text, magnificent as it is, that is specially important. A closer look at the illustration will show that between the lines of Latin there is some small writing in a very different style. This is a paraphrase translation of the Latin text into Anglo-Saxon, made in about A.D. 950 by Aldred, and its importance lies in the fact that it is the earliest known translation of the gospels into the language of the English people.

# 3 ENGLISH VERSIONS

## JOHN WYCLIFFE

This portrait (**125**) of John Wycliffe is copied from a tablet in King's College, Cambridge. Wycliffe and his followers gave us the first complete Bible in English. His New Testament was completed about the year 1380 (about 70 years before the invention of printing) and is now in the British Museum. A page of Wycliffe's work is illustrated (**126**). The illuminated capital letter seven lines from the top of the first column begins John 5. The text is not difficult to read if it is remembered that 'y' is the same as our 'th'. Although Wycliffe's is not a very good translation, he began the process which made it possible for the Bible to be read by the ordinary people of England. There are about 170 manuscript copies still in existence, most of them in the revised form that was prepared soon after the death of Wycliffe.

**125** *Portrait of John Wycliffe: King's College, Cambridge, England*

**126** *Wycliffe's New Testament: British Museum, London*

**127** *Portrait of William Tyndale: from an oil painting by an unknown artist in Hertford College, Oxford, England*

**128** *Tyndale's New Testament: British and Foreign Bible Society Library, London*

## WILLIAM TYNDALE

Discouraged by the Church authorities of his day from working in England, Tyndale (**127**) eventually produced the first printed copies of the New Testament in English at Worms in Germany in 1525. His was a translation from the original Greek, unlike Wycliffe's which was made from the Latin Vulgate then in universal use. Copies of Tyndale's New Testament imported into England were burnt at such places as Paul's Cross in London, but the time came when more copies were pouring into the country than were being burnt. Nevertheless, only two copies of the original 6,000 copies of Tyndale's New Testament are still in existence; a complete copy now in the Baptist College, Bristol, and a mutilated copy in the library of St Paul's Cathedral.

The illustration (**128**) shows the first page of Matthew's gospel. Notice the black-letter type (also called 'Gothic'), and the small picture at the beginning of the first verse showing Matthew writing his gospel, with an angel dictating or supervising the writing over his shoulder. There is a longish note in the right margin.

MILES COVERDALE

Miles Coverdale (**129**) produced the first complete English printed Bible. It was printed abroad, probably at Marburg, and appeared in 1535. It was the first English Bible to be circulated in England with official support from the Church. The text of the New Testament (**130**) is largely a revision of Tyndale's work by comparison with Luther's German version.

**129** *Portrait of Miles Coverdale*

**130** *Coverdale's New Testament: Brtish and Foreign Bible Society Library, London*

# The gospel
## of S. Mathew.

The first Chapter.

Luc.3.d
Gen.21.a
Gen.25.c
Gen.29.f
Gen.38.e
Gen.46.b
Ruth.4.d
1.Par.2.a
Num.1.a
1.Reg.16.a
2.Re.11.c
1.Par.3.b
2.Re.11.g
2.Par.20.d
2.Pa.27.b
2.Par.28.d
4.Re.20.c
4.Re.21.d
4.Re.21.e
4.Re.22.f
24.25
1.Par.3.c
Agg.1.a
1.Eld.3.2

This is the boke of the generacion of Jesus Christ ye sonne of Dauid, the sonne of Abraham. Abrahã begat Isaac: Isaac begat Jacob: Jacob begat Judas z his brethrẽ: Judas begat Phares z Zarã of Thamar: Phares begat Hesrom: Hesrom begat Aram: Aram begat Aminadab: Aminadab begat Naasson: Naasson begat Salmon: Salmon begat Boos of Rahab: Boos begat Obed of Ruth: Obed begat Jesse: Jesse begat Dauid the kynge:

Dauid the kynge begat Salomon, of her that was the wyfe of Vry: Salomon begat Roboam: Roboam begat Abia: Abia begat Asa: Asa begat Josaphat: Josaphat begat Joram: Joram begat Osias: Osias begat Joatham: Joatham begat Achas: Achas begat Ezechias: Ezechias begat Manasses: Manasses begat Amon: Amon begat Josias: Josias begat Jechonias and his brethren aboute the tyme of the captiuyte of Babylon.

And after the captiuyte of Babylon, Jechonias begat Salathiel: Salathiel begat Zorobabel:

Zorobabel begat Abiud: Abiud begat Eliachim: Eliachim begat Azor: Azor begat Sadoc: Sadoc begat Achin: Achin begat Eliud: Eliud begat Eleasar: Eleasar begat Matthan: Matthan begat Jacob: Jacob begat Joseph the hußbande of Mary, of whõ was borne that Jesus, which is called Christ.

All the generacions from Abrahã to Dauid are fourtene generacions: From Dauid vnto the captiuite of Babylon, are fourtene generacions. From the captiuite of Babylon vnto Christ, are also fourtene generacions.

C
Luc.1.b
Some reader before they sat at home together.

The byrth of Christ was on thys wyse: When his mother Mary was maried to Joseph * before they came together, she was foũde with chylde by ye holy goost. But Joseph her hußbande was a perfect man, and wolde not brynge her to shame, but was mynded to put her awaie secretely. Neuertheles whyle he thus thought, beholde, the angell of the LORDE appered vnto him in a dreame, saynge: Joseph thou sonne of Dauid, feare not to take vnto the Mary thy wyfe. For that which is cõceaued in her, is of ye holy goost. She shall brynge forth a sonne, and thou shalt call his name Jesus. For he shall saue his people from their synnes.

Phi.2 a
Act.4.a

All this was done, ye the thinge might be fulfilled, which was spoken of the LORDE by the prophet, saynge: Beholde, a mayde shall be with chylde, and shall brynge forth a sonne, and they shall call his name Emanuel, which is by interpretacion, God wt vs.

Esa.7.c

Now whan Joseph awoke out of slepe he did as the angell of ye LORDE bade hym, and toke his wyfe vnto hym, and knewe her not, tyll she had brought forth hir fyrst borne sonne, and called his name Jesus.

Luc.2.a

The II. Chapter.

When Jesus was borne at Bethleẽ in Jury, in the tyme of Herode the kynge, Beholde, there came wyse men from the east to Jerusalẽ, saynge: Where is the new borne kynge of the Jues? We haue sene his starre in the east, and are come to worship him.

When Herode ye kynge had herde thys, he was troubled, z all Jerusalẽ with hym, and he gathered all the hye prestes and Scribes of ye people, z axed of them, where Christ shulde be borne. And they sayde vn-

### AUTHORIZED VERSION OR KING JAMES BIBLE

The Authorized Version appeared in 1611, and its production was one of the most important events in the reign of James I. The work was done by about 50 of the leading Biblical scholars of the day, and the influence of this version, 'the most majestic thing in our literature', upon our speech and way of life is incalculable.

The illustration (**131**) shows a copy of the Authorized Version of 1611 open at the first chapter of Matthew's gospel. The spelling is, of course, that of the seventeenth century, and modern copies of the Authorized Version have had the spelling revised and the ornate decoration removed.

**131** *Authorized Version*

# Christian Art

# Christian Signs
and Symbols

JESSE'S STEM

This ivory panel (**132**) is a typical example of a Jesse's stem. Similar representations are sometimes seen in stained glass windows. Jesus was 'born of David's stock' (Rom. 1 : 3), and David was a 'son of Jesse' (1 Sam. 16: 18). The family tree from Jesse to Jesus is therefore important (**196**). In this panel Jesse is reclining, and a tree is springing out of his heart ('a shoot out of the stock of Jesse' (Isa. 11: 1)). The kings of the line of David, wearing their crowns and with sceptres in their hands, occupy the branches of the tree, and at the top Mary sits holding Jesus on her knee. Rays of light like the rays of the sun proceed from the figures of Mary and Jesus, as if to give them greater prominence.

**132** *Jesse's stem: ivory panel: British Museum, London*

**133** *Adoration of the Shepherds, Ghirlandajo, fifteenth century: Galleria Antica e Moderna, Florence*

## JESUS AS A CHILD

The three illustrations **133**, **134** and **135** may usefully be studied together. Ghirlandajo's Nativity (**133**) shows Jesus lying naked and helpless like any other new-born baby, but the artist has given him a halo to remind us of his divinity, and the cross on the halo hints already at the suffering Jesus must eventually endure.

Rossellino's terracotta statue (**134**) depicts a normal child, happy and contented, with no indication of either his divinity or his future destiny, and it is the mother's deep affection for her child that shines out most clearly in this work.

Henry Moore's sculpture (**135**) by its massive simplicity brings out the eternal wonder of perfect motherhood and perfect childhood seen in the mystery of the Incarnation, and at the same time manages also to foreshadow in the expressions on the faces of the mother and the child the pain each will have to bear.

Notice how Ghirlandajo depicts the three shepherds, in attitudes suggesting wonder, reverence and service. Notice also the procession of dignitaries through a triumphal arch, representing the homage due to Christ from the great ones of the earth as well as from poor shepherds; the awe-struck Joseph, mystified by all that is happening; Mary in an attitude of deep devotion to her child; flowers springing up where the child lies; and the 'manger' which looks more like a tomb than a cradle, in anticipation of the death of Christ.

In the Rossellino and Moore statues the child is held by his mother; and in the Moore he sits in regal state, a king already, enthroned on the living throne of a mother's knee.

**134** *Mother and Child, Rossellino, fifteenth century: Victoria and Albert Museum, London*

**135** *Mother and Child, Henry Moore, twentieth century: St Matthew's Church, Northampton, England*

**136** *Flight into Egypt, Master of the Mondsee, fifteenth century: Museum of Medieval Austrian Art, Vienna*

THE FLIGHT INTO EGYPT

In both these pictures Joseph leads the animal on which the mother and child are riding. In the medieval picture (**136**) he is walking with a determined stride and a forward look towards his destination; in the Chinese picture (**137**) he is looking back and giving words of encouragement and reassurance to Mary as they are about to ford a wide river. In both pictures Joseph carries provisions for the journey. These artists portray, in widely different settings, the same tender concern of the mother for her child and the same determination on the part of Joseph to reach a place of safety for his family. The guardian angels keeping a discreet distance in the tree-tops are characteristic of medieval art, but the decorative, star-spangled sky is rather unusual.

**138** *Finding of Jesus in the Temple, Holman Hunt, nineteenth-twentieth centuries: City of Birmingham Art Gallery*

### THE FINDING OF JESUS IN THE TEMPLE

William Holman Hunt belonged to the Pre-Raphaelite Brotherhood, whose members aimed at reproducing in their work the strictest possible realism. Before painting the religious pictures by which he is best known, Holman Hunt visited Palestine in search of background information. He then crowded as much of this information as possible into the pictures he painted. This picture (**138**) is a good example of Pre-Raphaelite realism.

Notice the rabbi on the left wearing his tallit (**80**) and holding a scroll of the law in his arm; the rabbi next to him holding a small scroll in his hand (probably a scroll of Esther, the book read at the Jewish festival of Purim); the musical instruments held by the players in the background on the left; the magnificence of Herod's temple, and the work of construction still in progress.

**139** *Baptism of Jesus, Piero della Francesca, fifteenth century: National Gallery, London*

THE BAPTISM

The earliest pictures of this incident (Matt. 3 : 13–17) show Jesus being baptized by immersion in the Jordan, but both these works represent his baptism by aspersion (i.e. sprinkling water on the head from a shell or a basin). Piero della Francesca's painting (**139**) shows a shallow winding stream in which the background scenery is reflected and in which Jesus and John are standing. The colours in the original are cool and bright. The man in the background is Jesus undressing in readiness for his baptism, the artists' common trick of showing two stages of an action as if they were going on simultaneously. The 'Spirit of God descending like a dove' (Matt. 3 : 16) is represented literally by a white dove (**180**) hovering over the head of Christ.

The African bronze statue (**140**) in its simplicity shows Jesus, who needed no 'baptism in token of repentance, for the forgiveness of sins' (Mark 1 : 4), meekly submitting to John's ministry. The expression on John's face is one of perplexity, reflecting his words to Jesus: 'I need rather to be baptized by you' (Matt. 3 : 14). The artist has put a cross in John's hand, thus carrying our thought forward to that other baptism Christ had to endure and of which he spoke when he said, 'I have a baptism to undergo, and how hampered I am until the ordeal is over!' (Luke 12 : 50). In this statue John stands much taller than Jesus, but this surely is not intended to suggest superiority, for John once said of Jesus: 'As he grows greater, I must grow less' (John 3 : 30), a quotation Grünewald has contrived to include in Latin behind the figure of John the Baptist in his famous picture of the Crucifixion (**150**).

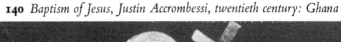

**140** *Baptism of Jesus, Justin Accrombessi, twentieth century: Ghana*

### PORTRAITS OF JESUS

The early Church was more concerned with symbols (pp. 144–56) than with portraits and no genuine portrait of Jesus, or even a description in words of his physical appearance, is known to exist. Although we shall therefore never know what Jesus really looked like, artists have often tried to imagine his appearance and to depict it. Two of these attempts, one ancient and the other modern, are represented here. The ancient portrait was painted not later than about A.D. 150 on the ceiling of the tomb of Saints Achilleus and Nereus in the catacombs at Rome. The illustration shown here (**141**) is a copy, made by Thomas Heaphy about 1847, of the painting in the tomb. The original is much faded and although the copyist worked with great care it is by no means certain that his copy closely resembles the original or that the original was a genuine likeness of Jesus.

Rouault's picture (**142**) makes no attempt to produce a portrait as near as possible to the actual appearance of Christ; the artist has tried instead to put into the expression on the face all the sorrow that Christ bore and all the yearning, compassion and love that he felt. In this way he has succeeded in conveying the essential truth about Christ.

**141** *Portrait of Jesus, in the catacombs, Rome: this copy of it is in the British Museum, London*

**144** *Last Supper, Leonardo da Vinci, fifteenth–sixteenth centuries: Convent of St Maria delle Grazie, Milan*

### THE LAST SUPPER

'On the night of his arrest' (1 Cor. 11:23) Jesus 'sat down with the twelve disciples' (Matt. 26:20) to eat with them the Passover supper (only the synoptic gospels say it was the Passover meal: John says otherwise (**200**)). When he announced that one of them would betray him, 'in great distress they exclaimed one after the other, "Can you mean me, Lord?"' (Matt. 26:20–5). This is the moment captured by Leonardo da Vinci and Riemenschneider in the works illustrated here. Riemenschneider (**143**) shows Judas standing in the centre of the group saying, 'Rabbi, can you mean me?', but Leonardo (**144**) shows him seated, his face in gloomy shadow. In both cases Judas holds 'the common purse, which was in his charge' (John 12:6), or perhaps a purse containing the 'thirty silver pieces' (**96**) which the chief priests had already 'weighed him out' as a reward for his betrayal of Jesus into their hands (Matt. 26:14–16).

Leonardo's original painting on the wall of a convent refectory in Milan has almost disappeared, and what is seen today is largely the work of later restorers.

**143** *Last Supper, Riemenschneider, fifteenth–sixteenth centuries: middle panel of the 'Blood Altar', Rothenburg, Germany*

Spencer's picture (**145**) shows greater spiritual insight and really gets to the heart of the matter in a way the others fail to do, for it is not what the disciples thought, but what Jesus *did* that is of supreme importance on this occasion. That is why Spencer concentrates attention on the institution of the Eucharist rather than on the identification of Judas as the betrayer. Paul thus describes the moment depicted in Spencer's painting: 'the Lord Jesus, on the night of his arrest, took bread and, after giving thanks to God, broke it and said: "This is my body, which is for you; do this as a memorial of me." ' (1 Cor. 11 : 23–4). The scene is represented most movingly. The disciples look mystified, perhaps incredulous, and one of them is gazing rather foolishly into the middle of the broken loaf to see if it *has* been changed into the 'body' of Christ. Looking at this picture it is easy to recognize the dramatic significance and the religious importance of the incident it depicts.

Spencer's picture was painted in 1920. The brick walls and the window which form the modern setting of this work are probably copied from a building in Cookham, Spencer's native Thames-side village, but the *triclinium* (or three-sided table) is very much like the tables used for formal meals in New Testament times. It is easy to see how at this sort of table it would be possible for Jesus to 'wash his disciples' feet' (John 13 : 3–5), and for the 'woman who was living an immoral life in the town' to bring

**145** *Last Supper, Stanley Spencer, nineteenth-twentieth centuries:*
*Holy Trinity Church, Cookham-on-Thames, Berkshire, England*

'oil of myrrh in a small flask' to a dinner at the house of 'one of the Pharisees' and to wet Jesus's feet with her tears, wipe them with her hair, kiss them and anoint them with the myrrh (Luke 7: 36–8). In one respect this picture might give a wrong impression. Guests at a meal probably reclined on one elbow, with their feet pointing *away* from the table, and this must be why Luke says the woman 'took her place behind him, by his feet' (Luke 7: 37).

**146** *Christ Washing Peter's Feet, Ford Madox Brown, nineteenth century: Tate Gallery, London*

Ford Madox Brown has a picture of the foot-washing incident (**146**). It shows Peter, having first protested against it, now submitting to have his feet washed by Jesus. The folded hands and the bowed head are expressive of Peter's complete submission to Christ, while the other disciples look on in amazement and one of them prepares to take his turn after Peter. The outstanding impression made by this picture is of the intense emotion that marked this incident in Christ's ministry.

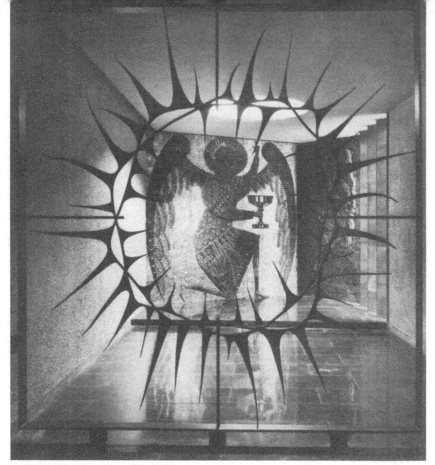

**147** *Chapel of Christ in Gethsemane, Basil Spence, twentieth century: Coventry Cathedral, England*

### GETHSEMANE

The wrought-iron screen of the Chapel of Christ in Gethsemane in Coventry Cathedral (**147**) was designed by Sir Basil Spence, the architect of the cathedral, and made in the workshops of the Royal Engineers at Chatham. It is in the form of a crown of thorns, and the reredos (the wall behind the altar) seen through the screen depicts 'an angel from heaven bringing him strength' (Luke 22 : 43). The angel holds the cup about which Jesus prayed : 'Father, if it be thy will, take this cup away from me. Yet not my will but thine be done' (Luke 22 : 42). The mosaic on the right portrays the sleeping disciples, 'worn out by grief' (Luke 22 : 45).

### THE CRUCIFIXION

Roman law compelled criminals condemned to death by crucifixion to carry their cross to the place of execution. The synoptic gospels say that at Jesus's crucifixion they 'seized upon a man called Simon, from Cyrene' and 'put the cross on his back, and made him walk behind Jesus carrying it' (Luke 23 : 26) but John says that Jesus was 'taken in charge and, carrying his own cross, went out to the Place of the Skull . . . where they crucified him' (John 19 : 17).

Both the artists whose work is shown here have accepted John's account rather than that of the synoptics. Schongauer's engraving (**148**) depicts a bustling crowd surrounding Jesus; Accrombessi's deeply moving statue (**149**) represents Jesus as a lonely, pathetic figure. In the engraving Christ has fallen under the weight of his cross and is being lashed by a soldier to urge him on. The swords and spears of the soldiers are much in evidence. In the statue Jesus is still on his feet, but one arm has already released its hold on the cross (which is being carried, unusually, on the back) and he seems about to fall. Notice how Accrombessi has used the elongated neck, the position of the feet, and the expression on the face to emphasize the physical torture in this incident in the story of the Passion of Christ.

**148** *Christ Carrying his Cross, Schongauer, fifteenth century: British Museum, London*

**149** *Christ Carrying his Cross, Justin Accrombessi, twentieth century: Ghana*

The earliest known picture of the Crucifixion is a crudely drawn blasphemous caricature preserved in the Kircher Museum, Rome, in which Christ is drawn with an ass's head. The sense of humiliation associated with crucifixion was very real to the early Christians, and it was not until the fifth century that Christian artists dared to portray Christ on the cross between two thieves. From this time onward, however, the Crucifixion was a favourite subject, and many of the world's greatest artists have produced representations of it.

Grünewald shows Jesus surrounded by his friends (**150**); Sutherland shows Jesus as a solitary figure suffering the agonies of crucifixion in complete loneliness (**151**). Neither the medieval nor the modern picture makes any attempt to minimize the horrors of crucifixion or to idealize the situation, as some painters have tended to do. The outstretched fingers, the distorted feet, the facial expression, and the drooping head of Christ all vividly portray the torment and the anguish of this form of death. Grünewald

**150** *Crucifixion, Grünewald, fifteenth–sixteenth centuries: Isenheim Altar, now in the Unterlinden Museum, Colmar, France*

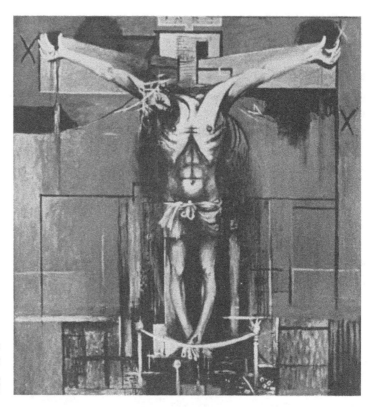

**151** *Crucifixion, Graham Sutherland, twentieth century: St Matthew's Church, Northampton, England*

adds to the horror of the scene by showing the flesh of Christ's body already in a state of putrefaction, although this contradicts the New Testament tradition (Acts 2 : 27, 31).

In Grünewald's picture Christ is shown to be both God and man. The bystanders on the left are sorrowing for the death of a human friend, and Mary is being comforted by John (John 19 : 25–7); John the Baptist on the right is pointing to Christ with an elongated finger as if acclaiming him the divine Saviour and saying: 'Look, there is the Lamb of God; it is he who takes away the sin of the world' (John 1 : 29). The inscription between John's head and his pointing finger is a Latin version of the words used by John of Christ: 'As he grows greater, I must grow less' (John 3 : 30). The figure of Christ on the cross is exaggerated in size, perhaps to symbolize the meaning of John's words (cf. **140**).

The 'Lamb of God' in symbolic form and bearing a cross (note the striking similarity to **156**) stands at the feet of John the Baptist. The letters INRI (**170**) are seen above the cross in both pictures. Grünewald's masterpiece is painted on the backs of the folding wings of an altar which when folded together form the picture shown here. The fronts of the wings have as subjects the Annunciation, the Virgin and Child, and the Resurrection.

CHRIST IN GLORY

Early on the Sunday morning following the Crucifixion some women 'came to the tomb bringing the spices they had prepared' to anoint the body of Jesus, but they saw that 'the stone had been rolled away from the tomb' and when they went inside the tomb 'the body was not to be found' (Luke 23 : 55—24 : 3). The Resurrection is an event in the gospel story too important to be ignored by artists, yet the Resurrection appearance of Christ is so difficult to depict that for a long time the subject was treated symbolically only (e.g. **171**). Eventually, however, attempts were made to give a representation of Christ rising from the tomb, and one of these attempts is shown here (**152**). The risen Christ is seen stepping out of a 'tomb' which bears no resemblance to a real Palestinian tomb (**92**). The sleeping soldiers are blissfully unaware of the momentous event that is being enacted. His one foot on the edge of the tomb gives Christ an almost defiant air and his face has a triumphant expression, but the wounds are visible in his hands, side and foot. He carries a flag of victory, but its sign is a cross. The two-fold mystery of Death and Resurrection (**169**) is thus never lost sight of in this picture.

**152** *Resurrection, Piero della Francesca, fifteenth century:*
*Galleria Comunale, Borgo San Sepolcro, Italy*

**153** *Ascension, Andrea Mantegna, fifteenth–sixteenth centuries: part of a triptych now in the Uffizi, Florence*

The Ascension presents even greater difficulties to an artist than does the Resurrection. The account of it in Acts simply says that Jesus 'was lifted up, and a cloud removed him from their sight', and that 'as they were gazing intently into the sky . . . two men in white' joined 'the apostles whom he had chosen' and told them that Jesus would return 'in the same way as you have seen him go' (Acts 1: 1–11).

In this picture of the Ascension (**153**) the artist has interpreted Luke's words quite literally, but he has also called upon the rich imagination for which he is famous and which characterizes all his work. The eleven disciples (thirteen can be counted; does this number include the 'two men in white' but not yet, of course, the successor of Judas Iscariot ?), two of them kneeling, are 'gazing intently into the sky'; Christ is being 'lifted up' by a host of cherubs; and an extremely formal cloud has 'removed him from their sight'. Christ bears a flag on which is the sign of the cross, signifying the victory he gained by his death (**152**), and his hand is held up in blessing on the astonished, awe-struck disciples.

Epstein's enormous aluminium statue (**154**) erected high above the nave in Llandaff Cathedral represents a mysterious figure of Christ. The use of a modern medium, aluminium, is intended to suggest that Christ is Lord also of the twentieth century. The extended hands reveal the wound marks, and suffering is expressed in the feet and the face and symbolized in the cross on the halo, yet the overall impression is one of majesty. This Christ has overcome the sharpness of death, but he is not yet fully glorified. He seems suspended between suffering on the one hand and glory on the other. The extended feet suggest ascension, but he is 'not yet ascended to the Father' (John 20: 17). The marks of authority, suffering and majesty in this magnificent figure remind us that Christ was a prophet of whom it could be said, 'No man . . . ever spoke as this man speaks' (John 7: 46); 'a high priest for ever in the succession of Melchizedek' (Heb. 6: 20); and a king, not only 'King of the Jews' as Pilate insisted (John 19: 19–22), but one who could say: 'My kingdom does not belong to this world. . . . My kingly authority comes from elsewhere' (John 18: 36).

**154** *Majestas, Jacob Epstein, nineteenth–twentieth centuries: Llandaff Cathedral, Wales*

**155** *Adoration of the Lamb, Jan van Eyck, fourteenth–fifteenth*
*centuries: St Bavon Cathedral, Ghent, Belgium*

Although the Ascension ended the earthly ministry of Christ, an important section
of Christian art goes beyond this event and attempts to portray 'the Son of Man
coming on the clouds of heaven with great power and glory' (Matt. 24: 30) or 'the
Son of Man . . . in his glory and all the angels with him' as he sits 'on his throne, with
all the nations gathered before him' (Matt. 25: 31–2). The vision of Christ in glory in
the Revelation of John has been a source of inspiration to musicians (e.g. Handel in the
great choruses in the final section of his *Messiah*) and artists, some of whom have tried
to reproduce the scene John saw through the 'door opened in heaven' (Rev. 4: 1). One
of the best known of these attempts is that of Jan van Eyck (**155**). This work is of great
artistic importance and interest, but it also reveals considerable religious insight on the
part of the artist.

'In the very middle of the throne, inside the circle of living creatures and the circle
of elders' stands 'a Lamb with the marks of slaughter upon him' (Rev. 5: 6). Christ is

represented in this picture as the sacrificial victim 'slain . . . since the world was made' (Rev. 13 : 8), whose blood did 'purchase for God men of every tribe and language, people and nation' (Rev. 5 : 9), who 'has won the right to open the scroll and break its seven seals' (**112**), and who is 'worthy . . . to receive all power and wealth, wisdom and might, honour and glory and praise!'. Surrounding the throne are the 'myriads upon myriads . . . thousands upon thousands' of those who are 'singing a new song' in adoration of the Lamb (Rev. 5 : 1–14). Patriarchs, prophets, saints, apostles and martyrs stand or kneel in four groups on a hillside with woods and fine buildings in the distance, a 'heaven' of the artist's imagination. The 'throne' is like an altar and blood is flowing from the wound in the body of the Lamb (**156**), to remind us of the words used by Jesus at the institution of the Eucharist: 'For this is my blood . . . shed for many for the forgiveness of sins' (Matt. 26 : 28). A cross with an inscription (**170**) is seen near the Lamb, to recall the historical event which this great work of art symbolizes.

**156** *Adoration of the Lamb: a detail*

**157** *Christ in Glory, Graham Sutherland, twentieth century: Coventry Cathedral, England*

The remarkable tapestry (**157**) which occupies the place of the 'east' window in Coventry Cathedral (actually the cathedral is built in a north–south position) is 78 feet long and 38 feet wide and weighs nearly a ton. It was designed by Graham Sutherland, made in France and presented anonymously to the cathedral by a resident of Coventry. It is rich in Christian symbolism.

Christ on the throne of his glory is the central figure. The marks of the nails in his feet are plainly visible and a Crucifixion, in which 'angels' on either side of the figure of Christ are hiding their faces from his suffering, is represented at the base of the tapestry. The two-fold idea of humiliation and glorification is thus forcibly brought out. A life-size figure of a man, stripped of the distinction that clothes might give him, stands between the pierced feet of Christ; and the descent of the Spirit in the form of a dove (**180**) is symbolically represented at the top of the tapestry. The 'four living creatures' (Rev. 4: 6–7), the lion, the ox, the man, and the eagle (**173–6**) surround the throne, and above the lion there is a representation of St Michael's victory over the Devil (**164**).

This gigantic figure of Christ in glory (the tapestry is the largest in one piece in the world) dominates the interior of the cathedral, reminding worshippers of the final victory of God in Christ, and of the voices 'heard in heaven shouting: "The sovereignty of the world has passed to our Lord and his Christ, and he shall reign for ever and ever!" ' (Rev. 11: 15).

### THE HOLY SPIRIT

Designed by John Piper and made by Patrick Reyntiens, the Baptistery window (**158**) is one of the most impressive features of Coventry Cathedral. The window is 85 feet high and weighs 3 tons. John Piper says of his design: 'I worked on the simplest of plans—a blaze of light, framed and islanded in rich colour. It is this blaze of light, symbolizing the Holy Spirit, that was the motive and has remained the focus, or formal point, of the design.' The frame of colour may represent the Church in the world, in which the Holy Spirit is always present as the source of beauty, truth and goodness wherever they are found.

**158** *Baptistery Window, John Piper, twentieth century: Coventry Cathedral, England*

FOLLOWERS OF JESUS

These panels (**159**) are the work of Albrecht Dürer. On the left are seen John and Peter, and on the right Mark and Paul. Peter holds a key to remind us that at Caesarea Philippi Jesus told him: 'I will give you the keys of the kingdom of Heaven' (Matt. 16: 19); and Mark holds a sword in his hand, perhaps suggesting that his gospel is the word of God, which 'cuts more keenly than any two-edged sword' (Heb. 4: 12); or perhaps as a reminder of the tradition that he was martyred by a sword. The books and the scroll symbolize the New Testament writings of Mark, John and Paul.

**159** *Four Apostles, Albrecht Dürer, fifteenth–sixteenth centuries:*
*Bavarian State Art Collection, Munich*

**160** *The Teacher, from the sarcophagus of Junius Bassus,*
*prefect of Rome, died* A.D. 358: *Vatican, Rome*

This sculpture (**160**) appears on a sarcophagus (i.e. a stone coffin). The figures are thought to represent Christ, in the centre, handing to Peter, on the right, a scroll of the law. The figure on the left is thought to be Paul. The faces of Peter and Paul depicted here are similar to those found in early works of art elsewhere, and it is just possible that this tradition is based on an authentic impression of the appearance of the two apostles (cf. **159**).

CONVERSION OF SAINT PAUL

This picture (**161**) shows the scene described in Acts 22: 6–11, in which Paul hears a voice and sees a vision and falls to the ground blinded by the light that 'flashed from the sky'. The dazed onlookers fell back, half blinded by the same light.

Michelangelo was obsessed with the strength of the human body, and the anatomy of the figures in this picture well illustrates this obsession. But because he was also profoundly Christian, Michelangelo knew that the power of God is greater than the strength of man, and this overwhelming power is seen here overcoming and humiliating man. It is shown in physical terms, but the artist surely intends it to have a meaning that is more than physical. The terrific energy of the horse running away in terror adds to the drama of the occasion, and the groups of floating figures in the sky suggest that this moment in history had significance in heaven as well as on earth.

**161** *Conversion of St Paul, Michelangelo, fifteenth–sixteenth centuries: Vatican, Rome*

**162** *St John the Evangelist on the Island of Patmos, Velazquez,
seventeenth century: National Gallery, London*

JOHN THE SEER

This picture (**162**) of John on 'the island called Patmos' (Rev. 1 : 9), by the Spanish
painter Velazquez, shows John as a young man writing down an account of the vision
he saw through the 'door opened in heaven' (Rev. 4 : 1).

**163** *Four Horsemen of the Apocalypse, Albrecht Dürer, fifteenth–sixteenth centuries: British Museum, London*

## THE FOUR HORSEMEN OF THE APOCALYPSE

Dürer's *Four Horsemen of the Apocalypse* (**163**) is one of a series of woodcuts which first appeared in 1489. The four horsemen are vividly represented in harsh outline in the picture but, although tragedy is everywhere to be seen, the artist has managed to avoid any suggestion of unnecessary crudity or coarseness. The woodcut is, of course, in black-and-white, but in the Revelation colour plays an important part in the scene.

The first horse is white, and its rider holds a bow; the second is red, and its rider wields 'a great sword'; the third is black, and its rider holds 'a pair of scales'; the fourth is 'sickly pale', and its rider's name is Death. The first rider 'rode forth, conquering and to conquer'; the second 'was given power to take peace from the earth and make men slaughter one another'; the third symbolized famine; and the fourth was given 'the right to kill by sword and by famine, by pestilence and wild beasts' (Rev. 6: 1–8). Lightning striking down from heaven adds terror to the already frightening scene. It is an awesome picture, unrelieved by any hopeful sign, of the terrifying national and personal calamities to which the people of God were exposed, or expected to be exposed, during the period of the Roman persecution of the Church.

## ST MICHAEL AND THE DEVIL

There are two references to Michael in the New Testament (Jude 9 and Rev. 12: 7–9), and in both of them Michael is in conflict with the Devil. In Jude he is described as 'the archangel Michael . . . in debate with the devil, disputing the possession of Moses's body' (an allusion to a legend in an apocryphal work known as the *Assumption of Moses*); and in the Revelation passage 'Michael and his angels' wage war with 'the dragon and his angels', and the dragon is identified as 'that serpent of old that led the whole world astray, whose name is Satan, or the Devil'.

Epstein has combined these two ideas to create an arresting bronze statue (**164**) which has been placed on the east wall outside Coventry Cathedral. This huge figure of Michael (it is nearly 25 feet high and the wing-span is 23 feet) is the solitary figure described in the Jude passage, but all the symbolism of the Revelation passage has been worked into the representation of Michael's victory over the Devil. Michael is depicted powerfully. There is beauty and strength in his face, although the marks of suffering— the cost of warfare—are not absent. There is no arrogant expression of triumph— Epstein himself said he had tried to express in the face of Michael not triumph but compassion. By contrast, the Devil lies bound and defeated, his face expressing bewilderment and frustration in his humiliation by the archangel. The story of Michael and the Devil may be no more than a legend, but Epstein has used it most effectively to show the reality of the struggle that goes on between life and death, and to encourage belief in the ultimate victory of life and the final defeat of death.

**164** *St Michael and the Devil, Jacob Epstein, nineteenth–twentieth centuries: Coventry Cathedral, England*

THE FISH

There are several references to fish and fishing in the gospels, and this may be why Clement of Alexandria, towards the end of the second century, chose a fish as an emblem to be used by the Christian Church. There is, however, another possible reason for the choice. The Greek word for 'fish' is *ichthus*, and this word can be made into an acrostic, thus:

I    Iesous (Jesus; I in Greek is the same as J in English)
Ch   Christos (Christ)
Th   Theou (God's)
U    Uios (Son)
S    Soter (Saviour)

The fish symbol, therefore, once the secret is known, conveys a wealth of meaning: Jesus Christ, God's Son, Saviour.

Other interpretations of the fish symbol have been suggested, e.g. that it is an emblem representing baptism, but neither the origin nor the meaning of the symbol is known with certainty. It occurs frequently from the second century onward. The example shown (**165**) is an inscription on a tombstone of the second or third century A.D. *Ichthus*, written in uncials (p. 97) is the first word on the top line of the inscription (in Greek, Ch and Th are represented by single letters, *X* and *Θ*, and in uncial Greek U is like Y, and S is like C). In addition to two fish, this tombstone shows an anchor (**178**) and a laurel wreath of victory.

**165** *Fish symbol, on a tombstone of the second or third century: Museo Cristiano, Vatican, Rome*

**166** *IHS sign*

IHS

IHS

This monogram ((**166**) the letters are sometimes interwoven) is very often seen in church decoration, especially on the pulpit. It is occasionally written IHC, since S and C are only different forms of the same letter in the Greek alphabet. The letters are an abbreviation for 'Jesus'. 'Ιησοῦς is the Greek form of 'Jesus'. It becomes *ΙΗΣΟΥΣ* when written in Greek capital letters, and the first three letters are IHS if English capitals are substituted for Greek, the letter which seems to be H being a capital long E in Greek. The letters are sometimes taken to stand for *Jesus Hominum Salvator* (Jesus Saviour of men), but this is almost certainly a misunderstanding of the original meaning.

CHI-RHO

Examples of the Chi-Rho sign are of frequent occurrence in Christian art. Χριστός is Greek for 'Christ', and the first two letters of the word (three in English: Chr), often interwoven as a monogram, form the Chi-Rho sign, an abbreviation for 'Christ'. Χριστός is often correctly translated 'Messiah' in the New English Bible. This detail (**167**) from the decoration on the side of a sarcophagus (i.e. a stone coffin) dating from about A.D. 350 displays the Chi-Rho sign very clearly. The crown of thorns above the cross has become the laurel wreath of victory, within which the Chi-Rho symbol stands. The wreath is held by the beak of an imperial eagle, symbol of power, and supported by two doves, symbols of the soul. The soldiers who were on guard at the tomb are seen in an attitude of despair, for their prisoner has escaped. This panel is often called *Anastasis*, i.e. Resurrection, because it depicts the triumph of Christ over death rather than his defeat by crucifixion. Another sarcophagus (**172**) of the sixth century is decorated with several representations of the Chi-Rho sign within victory wreaths of immortality on the lid. On the front it is seen between the letters alpha and omega (p. 148), and associated with the peacock, emblem of paradise, and the vine, emblem of immortality. The Chi-Rho sign is also to be seen above the baptistery in the illustration of the cock symbol (**168**).

**167** *Chi-Rho sign, on a sarcophagus of about* A.D. 350: *Museo Lateranense, Rome*

THE COCK

Because of its habit of crowing at dawn the cock became the symbol of watchfulness,
especially watchfulness for the Parousia (p. 174): 'Evening or midnight, cock-crow or
early dawn—if he comes suddenly, he must not find you asleep' (Mark 13 : 35–6). It
is, however, the association of the cock with Peter's denial that has established it as a
Christian symbol and kept it in popular use until today. Jesus had warned Peter, 'I tell
you, tonight before the cock crows you will disown me three times', but Peter strongly
refuted the possibility. Nevertheless, when 'a serving-maid', 'another girl' and later
'the bystanders' challenged him he denied the charge, and 'at that moment the cock
crew' (Matt. 26 : 31–5, 69–75).

The illustration (**168**) shows the carving on one side of a sarcophagus (or stone coffin)
of about A.D. 350. Jesus, on the left, holds up three fingers in prediction of Peter's
three-fold denial, and the cock stands on a pedestal between Peter and Jesus. On the
extreme left is a baptistery with the Chi-Rho sign (**167**) surmounting it, and its door
flung open, perhaps to signify the forgiveness, through baptism, of sin, even the sin of
denying Christ.

The weather-cocks commonly seen on church towers today are a reminder to those
who go to church, or pass by, of Peter's sin, and a warning of the danger of falling into
the same sin themselves.

**168** *Cock symbol, on a sarcophagus: Museo Lateranense, Rome*

169 *Cross, Richard Batty, twentieth century: Moorlands Methodist Church, Dewsbury, England*

170 *Inscription in Hebrew, Latin and Greek*

ישוע־דמן נצרת מלכא דיחודיא

JESVS·NAZARENVS·REX: JVDAEORVM

IHCOYC·O·NAZΩPAIOC·O·BACIΛEYC·TΩN·IOYΔAIΩN

## THE CROSS

The cross was probably the earliest sign to be used by Christians (but see p. 129), and it is still the symbol most frequently seen in Christian art and craftsmanship. This cross (169) was designed and made by Richard Batty. It is rich in meaning. 'Christ's cup of suffering' (2 Cor. 1 : 5) is vividly symbolized in the cruelly represented 'crown of thorns' (Matt. 27 : 29) and the nails (three nails, perhaps representing the Trinity). Jesus 'has been raised again, as he said he would be' (Matt. 28 : 6), for there is no figure on the cross now. The arms of the cross are slightly raised upward and slightly projected forward as if in invitation: 'Come to me, all whose work is hard, whose load is heavy; and I will give you relief' (Matt. 11 : 28), and again: 'I shall draw all men to myself, when I am lifted up from the earth' (John 12 : 32). For the inscription above the cross see 170.

## INRI

The letters I N R I are the initial letters of the Latin 'inscription to be fastened to the cross' that Pilate wrote: *Iesus Nazarenus Rex Iudaeorum*, 'Jesus of Nazareth King of the Jews' (John 19 : 19). The inscription was written in Hebrew (by which is probably meant Aramaic, for it was the language commonly spoken by Jews in Palestine in Christ's time); in Latin, the official language of the Roman army and the administrative officers; and in Greek, the language spoken by Jews from other parts of the Mediterranean area, many of whom were in Jerusalem for the Passover celebration at the time of the Crucifixion. The illustration (170) shows what the inscription in the three languages may have looked like.

**171** *Lamb and flag*

## LAMB WITH FLAG

The lamb (**171**) has associations with the Old Testament idea of sacrifice and represents 'the Lamb of God . . . he who takes away the sin of the world' (John 1 : 29). The flag is the banner of victory and symbolizes Christ's victory in the Resurrection. The lamb and flag are sometimes seen together (**150**) and sometimes the lamb only is depicted (**156**). The lamb and flag emblem has been the 'seal' of the Moravian Church, certainly from the sixteenth century and probably as early as the fifteenth century.

## ALPHA AND OMEGA

Alpha and Omega, the first and last letters of the Greek alphabet, are often used as Christian signs. Sometimes they appear in their English equivalents, A and O (e.g. in the last verse of the carol, *Unto us is born a Son*). They are symbols of Christ, who said : 'I am the Alpha and the Omega, the first and the last, the beginning and the end' (Rev. 22 : 13). This sarcophagus (**172**; see also p. 145) has several examples of the Alpha and Omega signs associated with the Chi-Rho signs as part of its symbolic decoration.

**172** *Alpha and Omega, on a sarcophagus of the sixth century: Ravenna, Italy*

THE FOUR EVANGELISTS

The author of the Revelation borrowed very many ideas and quotations from the Old Testament, and his picture of the 'four living creatures': the lion, the ox, the eagle and the man (Rev. 4: 6–8), obviously owes something to Ezekiel's vision 'by the river Chebar' (Ezek. 1: 1–10). The early Church soon linked John's quartet of creatures with the writers of the four gospels, and various equations were suggested. Attempts were made to relate the characteristics of the gospels to those of the creatures, and one such identification is as follows:

Matthew = the man      Mark = the lion
Luke    = the ox         John = the eagle

**173, 174** *Evangelists, from the Book of Cerne: University Library, Cambridge, England*

**175, 176** *Evangelists, from the Book of Cerne: University Library, Cambridge, England*

This is illustrated on the pages of the Book of Cerne (**173–6**), a collection of prayers, of about the eighth century, once belonging to Cerne Abbey in Dorset.

Notice that all the creatures are winged. This may be intended to symbolize the divine commission given to the apostles (the Greek word *apostolos* means 'one sent on a mission'). In this scheme Matthew is represented as a man because his gospel emphasizes the human ancestry of Jesus; Mark by a lion because his gospel shows the royal dignity of Jesus; Luke by an ox because his gospel draws attention to the sacrificial aspect of Jesus's ministry; and John by an eagle because his gospel soars upwards and indicates the divine nature of Jesus. The eagle also suggests the heavenly source of the gospel, and this is why the lectern in church is often in the form of an eagle.

**177** *Ship symbol of the World Council of Churches*

## THE SHIP

The First Letter of Peter contains a reference to Noah's ark (1 Peter 3 : 18–21), and this may explain the use of a ship as a symbol of the Church. We still call part of a church the nave (Latin: *navis*, a ship). This symbol (**177**) was designed by a group of Christians in Germany during the Hitler régime and sent to the World Council of Churches as a sign of their belief that Christians throughout the world are 'all one person in Christ Jesus' (Gal. 3 : 28). The ship afloat on a troubled sea represents the Church carrying the faithful to salvation, and the mast makes the sign of the cross by which salvation comes to man. The Greek word *oikoumene* occurs about fifteen times in the New Testament, where it means 'the whole inhabited earth'. The oecumenical Church (**198**) is the whole Church throughout the world. The symbol therefore stands for 'the total mission of the whole Church to the whole life of man and to the whole world'.

## THE ANCHOR

A representation of an anchor is frequently seen on tombstones, especially those in the catacombs (underground burial places) in Rome. It may have been its likeness to a cross that suggested its use as a Christian symbol in the first place, but a more likely explanation is the reference to it by the author of Hebrews. He says 'the hope set before us . . . is like an anchor for our lives, an anchor safe and sure' (Heb. 6: 18–19). In this passage the anchor is a symbol of hope and steadfastness, and in the Church it soon became, especially, a symbol of the Christian hope of life after death.

This example (**178**) belongs to the beginning of the third century. Hesperos is presumably the name of the person buried there. The fish tombstone (**165**) also has an anchor inscribed on it.

**178** *Anchor symbol of the third century: catacombs, Rome*

**179** *Scallop shell: Chapel of Henry VII, Westminster Abbey, London*

SCALLOP SHELL

The references in the New Testament to James, son of Zebedee, are comparatively few. We know that he was called to be a disciple (Matt. 4: 21), that he was present at the Transfiguration (Matt. 17: 1), and in the garden of Gethsemane (Matt. 26: 37), and that he was martyred by Herod Agrippa I in A.D. 44 (Acts 12: 1-2). Beyond these few facts we know almost nothing else for certain. There are, however, a number of legends in which James has a prominent place. One of them says that he made many pilgrimages, one of which brought him to Compostella, and that he was the first to bring Christianity to Spain. Another legend says that James was buried at Compostella, or that his relics were taken there. Certainly Compostella became a famous place of pilgrimage. Its full name is Santiago de Compostella, which means St James of Compostella.

James is also frequently associated with a scallop shell, and the French still call a scallop shell 'la coquille de Saint Jacques'. This figure of James (**179**) shows him with a scallop shell in his hat. Again, there are many legends to account for this association. One of the more fantastic stories tells how the relics of James were miraculously conveyed to Spain in a marble ship from Jerusalem. A knight on horseback was watching the ship sail into port, but his horse took fright and plunged him into the sea. He managed to save himself by boarding the marble ship, but his clothes were found to be entirely covered with scallop shells. The shore near Compostella is said to abound in scallop shells, and a more likely story is that pilgrims gathered them and wore them in their hats as evidence of the genuineness of their journey and to command admiration. A scallop shell is often used for baptism by sprinkling (**139**).

DOVE

The dove is represented in Christian art as a symbol of the Holy Spirit, because at his baptism (**139**) Jesus 'saw the Spirit of God descending like a dove to alight upon him' (Matt. 3 : 16). A dove is sometimes put above the pulpit in church as a symbol of the inspiration of the preacher by the Holy Spirit. At Tewkesbury there is an interesting roof boss (**180**) showing the descent of the Holy Spirit on the day of Pentecost when the disciples 'were all together in one place' (Acts 2 : 1–4). Mary is here prominently represented among the apostles. The story of Pentecost does not say that Mary was present, suggesting rather that it was only the twelve (Acts 1 : 26); but Acts 1 : 14 says of the eleven, 'All these were constantly at prayer together, and with them a group of women, including Mary the mother of Jesus, and his brothers.' The artist has included Mary, but none of the other women nor the brothers of Jesus.

**180** *Dove: Tewkesbury, England*

### THE TRINITY

The doctrine of the Trinity is not definitely stated in the New Testament, but there are hints of it in a number of places. The disciples were told to 'baptize men everywhere in the name of the Father and the Son and the Holy Spirit' (Matt. 28 : 19), and the Second Letter of Paul to the Corinthians ends with the words: 'The grace of the Lord Jesus Christ, and the love of God, and fellowship in the Holy Spirit, be with you all' (2 Cor. 13 : 14).

This symbol of the Trinity (**181**) is sometimes seen in church, carved in wood or stone, or in a stained-glass window. It does not attempt to 'explain' the mystery of the Trinity, but it does describe one aspect of the doctrine in a graphic form.

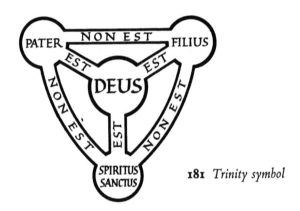

**181** *Trinity symbol*

### A CHRISTIAN ACROSTIC

This perfect word-square (**182**), is one of several similar examples found in various parts of the Roman Empire. One was unearthed in Pompeii, a city which was buried by a volcanic eruption in A.D. 79, and the one illustrated here was discovered in 1868 cut in the wall-plaster of a Roman house at Cirencester, the Roman city of Corinium, in Gloucestershire. If the inscription found at Pompeii is genuine and if the solution to the acrostic suggested here is the correct one, this may well be the earliest example of Christian writing known to us, perhaps as much as 70 years earlier than the Rylands fragment (**110**).

The word Arepo is unknown in Latin, but it may be a proper noun. If it is, a possible translation of the word-square would be: 'The sower Arepo holds the wheels carefully.' In 1926, Grosser, a German scholar, suggested that this word-square of 25 letters might be rearranged to form the first two words of the Lord's Prayer in Latin, in the shape of a cross, and with A and O (**172**) at the ends of the arms of the cross (**183**). This solution is not acceptable to all scholars, but no one has yet suggested a better one.

182 *Word-square of the fourth century: Corinium Museum, Cirencester, England*

183 *Word-square: a solution*

# Maps and Plans

# Charts and Diagrams

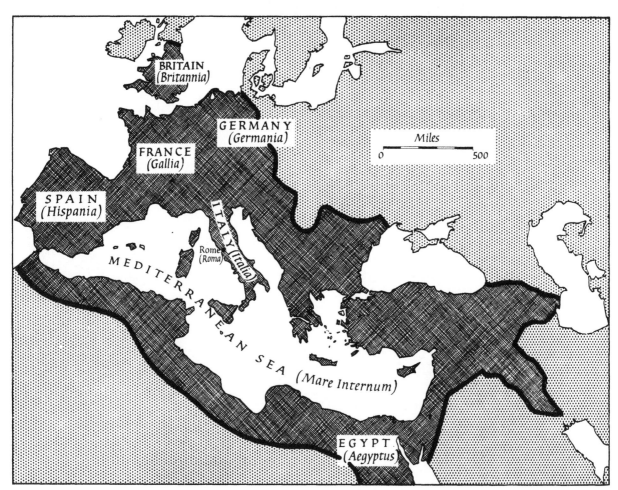

**184** *The Roman Empire*

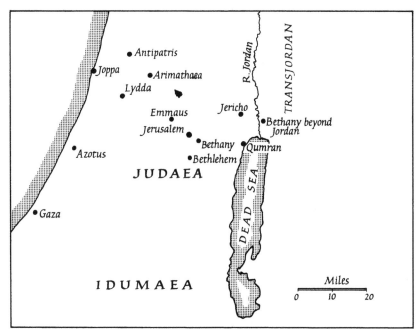

**185** *Judaea, the Dead Sea and Idumaea*

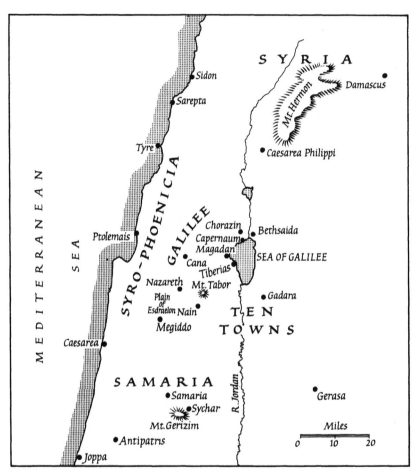

**186** *Galilee, Samaria, Phoenicia and Syria*

**187** *The Eastern Mediterranean*

**188** *Asia Minor*

**189** *Greece and Italy*

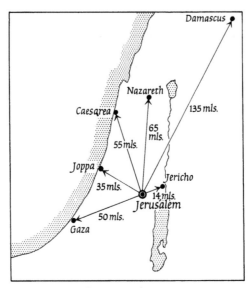

**190** *Distances from Jerusalem*

The distances shown on this map are 'as the crow flies'. Distances by road are much greater. For example, the traveller from Jerusalem to Jericho must cover a distance of about 21 miles.

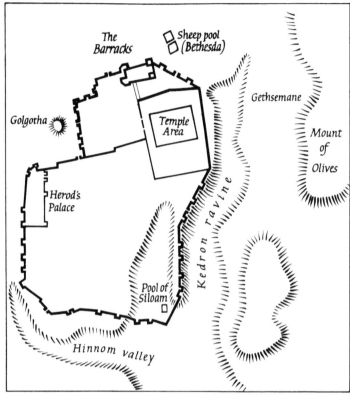

**191** *Jerusalem*

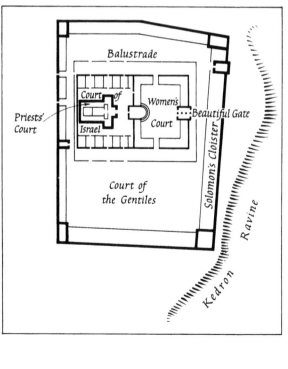

**192** *Herod's Temple and its precincts*

# CHARTS AND DIAGRAMS

## A TIME-CHART TO SHOW THE PLACE OF JESUS IN THE HISTORY OF RELIGION

The New Testament has a good deal to say about the place of Jesus in history. Luke fixes the time of Jesus's birth 'in the fifteenth year of the Emperor Tiberius, when Pontius Pilate was governor of Judaea, . . . during the high-priesthood of Annas and Caiaphas' (Luke 3 : 1–2). Both Matthew and Luke trace the ancestry of Jesus (see **196**): Matthew from Abraham (Matt. 1 : 1–17) and Luke from Adam (Luke 3 : 23–38). The opening words of the Letter to Hebrews say that 'when in former times God spoke . . . he spoke in fragmentary and varied fashion through the prophets', but that in 'the final age' he spoke 'in the Son whom he has made heir to the whole universe' (Heb. 1 : 1–2); and the Letter to the Galatians gives significance to the birth of Jesus by saying that it occurred 'when the term was completed' (Gal. 4 : 4).

The diagram (**193**) attempts to indicate this New Testament point of view and, in addition, to show the place of Jesus among some of the important figures in the Christian Church and the founders of some of the other religions of the world.

## A TIME-CHART OF THE NEW TESTAMENT

Precise dating of the events in the New Testament is impossible. The first column in the chart (**194**) must therefore be taken to mean only that here is the order and here are the probable dates of the events named. Similarly, it is impossible to date with certainty the books of the New Testament. The last column in the chart must therefore be understood to say only that here is a possible order and here are possible dates for the composition of the fifteen books named. The dates of the other twelve books in the New Testament are so uncertain that it is impossible to include them in the list.

The birth of Jesus is shown in the first column at a point somewhere between 10 and 5 B.C., and it may well be asked how Jesus could possibly be born in the era B.C. (i.e. before Christ). This is the explanation. Roman historians dated events from the foundation of the city of Rome, and this system of dating continued until the sixth century when Dionysius Exiguus calculated that the year 754 A.U.C. (i.e. *ab urbe condita*: from the foundation of the city) corresponded to the first year of the Christian era, A.D. 1. Since the time of Dionysius events in the Christian era have been dated on the basis of his calculation and this is the system we still use, but we know now that the calculation was about ten years wrong. One result of the error is that, on the basis of Dionysius's reckoning, the death of Herod must be dated 4 B.C., and since Jesus is known to have been born during Herod's reign (Matt. 2 : 1) his birth must have been a few years before 4 B.C.

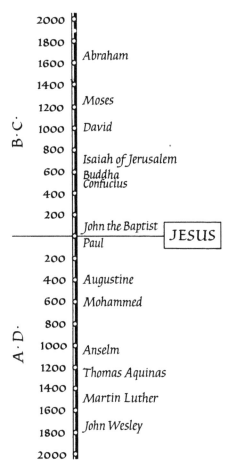

**193** *A time-chart to show the place of Jesus in the history of religion*

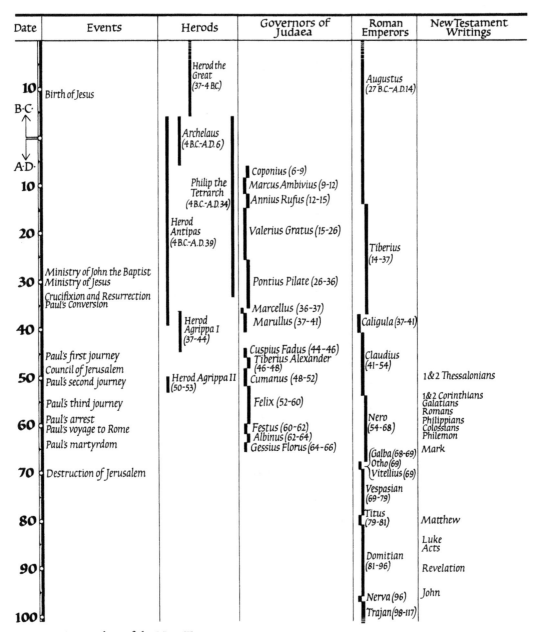

| Date | Events | Herods | Governors of Judaea | Roman Emperors | New Testament Writings |
|---|---|---|---|---|---|
| **10** B·C· | Birth of Jesus | Herod the Great (37-4 B.C.) | | Augustus (27 B.C.-A.D.14) | |
| A·D· | | Archelaus (4 B.C.-A.D. 6) | | | |
| **10** | | Philip the Tetrarch (4 B.C.-A.D.34) | Coponius (6-9) Marcus Ambivius (9-12) Annius Rufus (12-15) | | |
| **20** | | Herod Antipas (4 B.C.-A.D.39) | Valerius Gratus (15-26) | Tiberius (14-37) | |
| **30** | Ministry of John the Baptist Ministry of Jesus Crucifixion and Resurrection Paul's Conversion | | Pontius Pilate (26-36) | | |
| **40** | | Herod Agrippa I (37-44) | Marcellus (36-37) Marullus (37-41) | Caligula (37-41) | |
| **50** | Paul's first journey Council of Jerusalem Paul's second journey | Herod Agrippa II (50-53) | Cuspius Fadus (44-46) Tiberius Alexander (46-48) Cumanus (48-52) | Claudius (41-54) | 1 & 2 Thessalonians |
| **60** | Paul's third journey Paul's arrest Paul's voyage to Rome Paul's martyrdom | | Felix (52-60) Festus (60-62) Albinus (62-64) Gessius Florus (64-66) | Nero (54-68) | 1 & 2 Corinthians Galatians Romans Philippians Colossians Philemon Mark |
| **70** | Destruction of Jerusalem | | | Galba (68-69) Otho (69) Vitellius (69) Vespasian (69-79) | |
| **80** | | | | Titus (79-81) | Matthew Luke Acts |
| **90** | | | | Domitian (81-96) | Revelation John |
| **100** | | | | Nerva (96) Trajan (98-117) | |

**194** *A time-chart of the New Testament*

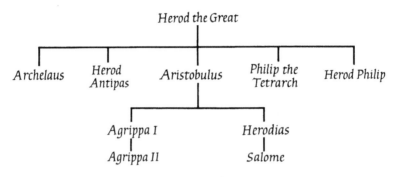

**195** *The Herod family in the New Testament*

THE HEROD FAMILY IN THE NEW TESTAMENT

Herod the Great had ten wives and many descendants, but this greatly simplified diagram (**195**) includes only those members of Herod's family who are of interest to students of the New Testament.

*Herod the Great* was king of Judaea, Galilee, Samaria and the land in the north-east of Palestine when Jesus was born 'at Bethlehem in Judaea' (Matt. 2: 1). He died in 4 B.C. (see p. 166 for a note on this date).

*Archelaus* inherited half the kingdom of his father, Herod the Great, and was king of Judaea when Joseph and Mary brought Jesus back from Egypt (Matt. 2: 22). The other half of Herod's kingdom was divided between Herod Antipas and Philip the Tetrarch. Originally a tetrarch was one who ruled a quarter of a country (*tetra* is a Greek prefix which means 'four'), but in later times a ruler who was not a king was sometimes called 'tetrarch' without reference to the size of his territory. Herod Antipas and Philip the Tetrarch were tetrarchs in the original sense.

*Herod Antipas* was 'prince of Galilee' when Jesus began his ministry (Luke 3: 1). 'Prince' is the word used to translate 'tetrarch' in the New English Bible. Herod Antipas is sometimes given the courtesy title 'King Herod' (e.g. Mark 6: 14). He wrongly married Herodias when her legal husband, Herod Philip, his half-brother, was still living (Matt. 14: 1–5).

*Philip the Tetrarch* was 'prince of Ituraea and Trachonitis' when Jesus began his ministry (Luke 3: 1). He is called 'Philip' in the New English Bible. He married Salome (see overleaf).

*Aristobulus* was the father of Agrippa I and Herodias. He is not mentioned in the New Testament (the Aristobulus mentioned in Rom. 16: 10 is a different person).

*Herod Philip* was the legal husband of Herodias (Matt. 14: 3). He, like Philip the Tetrarch, is called 'Philip' in the New English Bible.

*Agrippa I* beheaded James and imprisoned Peter (Acts 12: 1–5). He is called 'Herod' or 'King Herod' in the account of his persecution of the Church.

*Agrippa II* is called 'Agrippa' or 'King Agrippa' in the account of Paul's trial at Caesarea (Acts 25: 13—26: 32).

*Herodias* was the legal wife of Herod Philip, but she illegally married Herod Antipas (see above).

*Salome* was the daughter of Herodias. She is not specifically named in the New Testament, but we are told her name by the Jewish historian, Josephus. If the evidence of Josephus can be accepted it was Salome who danced before Herod Antipas and asked for the head of John the Baptist as a reward (Matt. 14: 6–11).

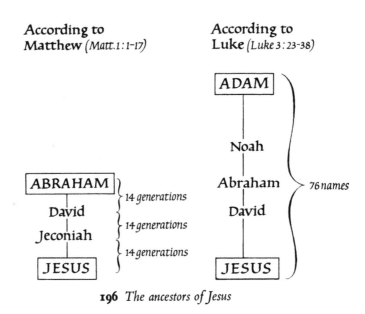

**196** *The ancestors of Jesus*

THE ANCESTORS OF JESUS

Matthew traces the descent of 'Joseph, the husband of Mary, who gave birth to Jesus called Messiah' (Matt. 1 : 16) through the royal line of Israel's kings back to Abraham, the father of the nation (**196**). Perhaps he intended to show that Jesus was the Messiah of his people, Israel, and that he could rightly be called 'the king of the Jews' (Matt. 27 : 37). The name David in its Hebrew form (DVD, omitting the vowels) is numerically equivalent to 4+6+4=14. The artificial arrangement of the names of Jesus's ancestors into three groups of 'fourteen generations' (Matt. 1 : 17) may be a hint of the importance of David in the line of descent.

Luke traces the descent of 'Jesus . . . the son, as people thought, of Joseph' (Luke 3 : 23) through a different line back to 'Adam, son of God' (Luke 3 : 38) (**196**). Perhaps he intended to show the kinship of Jesus with the whole human race, and to justify the title 'Son of Man' which Jesus seemed to prefer for himself.

The lists of ancestors given by Matthew and Luke agree from Abraham to David, but differ considerably from David to Joseph. In the latter section only Zerubbabel and Shealtiel occur in both lists.

References to women in Jewish lists of this kind are unusual, but Matthew mentions four: Tamar, Rahab, Ruth and Bath-sheba. The Jesse's stem in the British Museum (**132**) shows Mary in the position occupied by Joseph in the New Testament lists of Jesus's ancestors.


THE SYNOPTIC PROBLEM

Matthew, Mark and Luke are called synoptic gospels because they are so much alike in what they say and how they say it ('synoptic' comes from two Greek words meaning 'seen together'). Sometimes they agree word for word. But in spite of this similarity they also differ considerably from each other in some respects. Why is this? The diagram (**197**) shows one of the attempts to answer this question and to solve the 'synoptic problem'.

The areas of the rectangles roughly correspond to the number of verses in the various sections. M contains about 260 verses and is the material only Matthew had at his disposal. L contains about 600 verses and is the material only Luke had at his disposal. Q contains about 200 verses and is the material both Matthew and Luke had at their disposal (no one now knows for certain why it was called Q). Both Matthew and Luke also knew Mark's gospel, and Matthew used about 600 verses and Luke about 350 verses of Mark in compiling their own gospels. The material used by both Matthew and Luke accounts for the similarities; the material each used which the other did not use accounts for the differences.

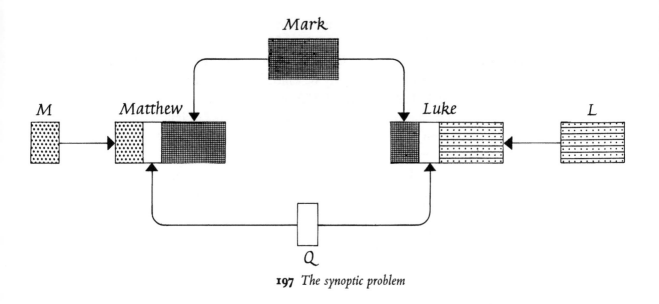

**197** *The synoptic problem*

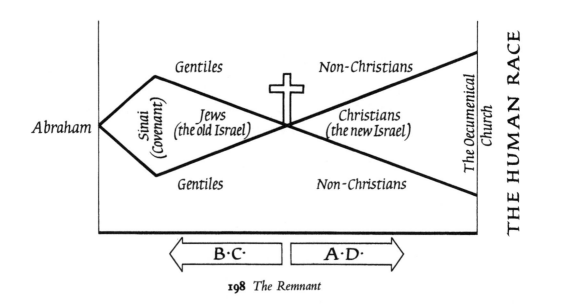

**198** *The Remnant*

THE REMNANT

The Old Testament contains a good deal of teaching about a 'remnant'—a righteous minority in whom lies Israel's hope of survival. The idea is less common in the New Testament, but it is not absent.

This diagram (**198**) is greatly over-simplified (history never moves in straight lines), but it shows how, beginning with Abraham and his family, the Hebrews increased in number until at Sinai the whole nation entered into covenant relationship with God; how the remnant dwindled during the rest of the Old Testament period, until at the Crucifixion Jesus's friends 'all deserted him and ran away' (Matt. 26: 56) and he remained alone to represent faithful Israel; and how the remnant—' "a remnant" . . . selected by the grace of God' (Rom. 11: 5)—has expanded since the Resurrection to constitute in our day the oecumenical Church (p. 151), although even this is no more than a minority movement in a vast non-Christian world.

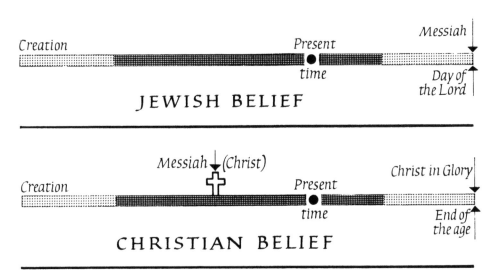

**199** *The coming of the Messiah according to the beliefs of Jews and Christians*

THE COMING OF THE MESSIAH ACCORDING TO THE BELIEFS OF JEWS AND
CHRISTIANS

Jews have always looked forward to the coming of the Messiah, and most Jews today
are still looking for his coming in the future. Some modern Jews, however, believe
that the Messiah came in a social form when the State of Israel was set up in 1948.

Christians agree with Peter when he said to Jesus, 'You are the Messiah' (Mark
8:29). 'Messiah', in its Hebrew form, and 'Christ', in its Greek form, mean exactly
the same; namely, 'the anointed one'.

The New Testament teaches that at 'the end of the age' (Matt. 24:3) Christ will
'appear a second time . . . to bring salvation to those who are watching for him'
(Heb. 9:28). Scholars use the Greek word for 'coming' and call this second coming
of Christ in glory the Parousia.

The chart (**199**) shows all this in a graphic form.


THE LAST SUPPER AND THE PASSOVER

The Jewish day begins and ends at sunset: our day begins and ends at midnight. The
diagram (**200**) makes the difference clear. The Crucifixion took place in the Jewish
month of Nisan, and all four gospels agree that the day was a Friday and that the day
between the Crucifixion and the Resurrection was a Saturday. The year in which the
Crucifixion took place is not known.

Nisan 14 was 'Preparation-day' (Mark 15:42) and the Passover lambs were
slaughtered during the afternoon of that day. The Passover meal was eaten during the
evening of (i.e. at the beginning of) Nisan 15. In the synoptic gospels the Last Supper
is the Passover meal: in John the Last Supper is eaten 24 hours before the time of the
Passover meal, and the Crucifixion takes place at the time of the slaughter of the Passover
lambs. All the events from the Last Supper to the burial of Christ occurred according
to the gospels during one day: between the evening of Maundy Thursday and the afternoon of Good Friday on our reckoning; on Nisan 15 according to the synoptic gospels,
and on Nisan 14 according to John. If we knew the year in which the Crucifixion
occurred we should be more likely to know the days of the week on which Nisan 14
and 15 fell.

## 1 According to the Synoptic Gospels

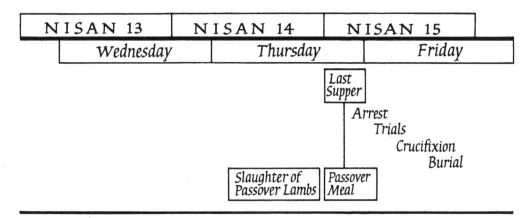

## 2 According to the Fourth Gospel

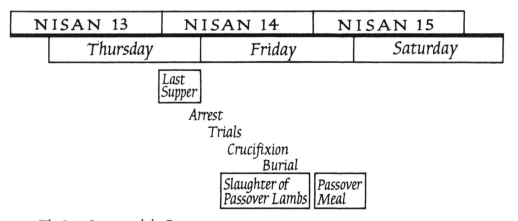

**200** *The Last Supper and the Passover*

# BIBLIOGRAPHY

THE BACKGROUND OF THE NEW TESTAMENT

BALY, D. *The Geography of the Bible*, Lutterworth Press, 1957

——*Palestine and the Bible*, Lutterworth Press, 1960

BEVAN, E. *Jerusalem under the High Priests*, Arnold, 1904

BOUQUET, A. C. *Everyday Life in New Testament Times*, Batsford, 1953

BOX, G. H. *Judaism in the Greek Period* (Vol. 5 of The Clarendon Bible), Oxford University Press, 1932

BROWNE, L. E. *From Babylon to Bethlehem*, Heffer, 1926

CAIRD, G. B. *The Apostolic Age*, Duckworth, 1955

CARPENTER, J. E. *Life in Palestine when Jesus Lived*, Lindsey Press, 1935

CORSWANT, W. *A Dictionary of Life in Bible Times*, Hodder and Stoughton, 1960

DEANE, A. C. *The World Christ Knew*, Eyre and Spottiswoode, 1944

DEURSEN, A. VAN *Illustrated Dictionary of Bible Manners and Customs*, Marshall, Morgan and Scott, 1958

FULLARD, H. (ed.) *Scripture Atlas*, Philip, 1962

GROLLENBERG, L. H. *Atlas of the Bible*, Nelson, 1956

——*Shorter Atlas of the Bible*, Nelson, 1959

HEDLUND, M. F. and ROWLEY, H. H. (eds.) *Atlas of the Early Christian World*, Nelson, 1958

HILLIARD, F. H. *Behold the Land*, Philip, 1963

KEE, H. C. and YOUNG, F. W. *The Living World of the New Testament*, Darton, Longman and Todd, 1960

KENYON, K. M. *Archaeology in the Holy Land*, Benn, 1965

LEANEY, A. R. C. *From Judaean Caves*, Religious Education Press, 1961

MATHEWS, B. *The World in which Jesus Lived*, Oxford University Press, 1937

MAY, H. G. (ed.) *Oxford Bible Atlas*, Oxford University Press, 1962

MILLER, M. S. and J. L. *Black's Bible Dictionary*, A. and C. Black, 1962

ROWLEY, H. H. *The Teach Yourself Bible Atlas*, English Universities Press, 1961

RUSSELL, D. S. *Between the Testaments*, S.C.M. Press, 1964

SMITH, J. W. D. *Bible Background*, Methuen, 1959

SNAITH, N. H. *The Jews from Cyrus to Herod*, Religious Education Press, 1963

TERRIEN, S. *Lands of the Bible*, Rathbone, 1957

UNGER, M. F. *Archaeology and the New Testament*, Pickering and Inglis, 1964

WISEMAN, D. J. *Illustrations from Biblical Archaeology*, The Tyndale Press, 1963

WRIGHT, G. E. *Biblical Archaeology*, Duckworth, 1962

WRIGHT, G. E. and FILSON, F. V. *The Westminster Historical Atlas of the Bible*, S.C.M. Press, 1958

THE GROWTH OF THE NEW TESTAMENT

DIAMOND, L. *How we got our Bible*, Oxford University Press, 1952

GRANT, R. M. *The Formation of the New Testament*, Hutchinson, 1965

HERKLOTS, H. G. G. *How the Bible Came to us*, Penguin Books (Pelican), 1959

KENYON, F. *The Story of the Bible*, John Murray, 1935

——*Our Bible and the Ancient Manuscripts*, Eyre and Spottiswoode, 1958

SPARKS, H. F. D. *The Formation of the New Testament*, S.C.M. Press, 1952

TAYLOR, V. *The Gospels: a Short Introduction*, Epworth Press, 1930


CHRISTIAN ART; CHRISTIAN SIGNS AND SYMBOLS

BRIDGE, A. C. *Images of God*, Hodder and Stoughton, 1960

COPE, G. *Symbolism in the Bible and the Church*, S.C.M. Press, 1959

——(ed.) *Christianity and the Visual Arts*, Faith Press, 1964

FERGUSON, G. *Signs and Symbols in Christian Art*, Hesperides, 1954

WATTS, A. J. *No New Thing*, S.P.C.K., 1949

——*Seeing Things*, S.P.C.K., 1959

# INDEX OF SUBJECTS

*Figures in bold type refer to illustrations*

# INDEX OF TEXTS

*Figures in italic type refer to pages*

For EU product safety concerns, contact us at Calle de José Abascal, 56–1°,
28003 Madrid, Spain or eugpsr@cambridge.org.

www.ingramcontent.com/pod-product-compliance
Ingram Content Group UK Ltd.
Pitfield, Milton Keynes, MK11 3LW, UK
UKHW030856150625
459647UK00021B/2784